growing berries and currants

a directory of varieties and how to cultivate them successfully

Richard Bird
and **Kate Whiteman**

LORENZ BOOKS

First published by Lorenz Books in 2002

Lorenz Books is an imprint of
Anness Publishing Limited
Hermes House
88–89 Blackfriars Road
London SE1 8HA

Published in the USA by
Lorenz Books
Anness Publishing Inc.
27 West 20th Street
New York, NY 10011

www.lorenzbooks.com

This edition distributed in Canada by
General Publishing
895 Don Mills Road,
400–402 Park Centre,
Toronto, Ontario M3C 1W3

A CIP catalogue record for this book is available from the British Library.

Publisher: Joanna Lorenz
Managing Editor: Judith Simons
Senior Editor: Doreen Palamartschuk
Art Manager: Clare Reynolds
Editor: Lydia Darbyshire
Additional text: Peter McHoy
Editorial Reader: Penelope Goodare
Photographers: Don Last, William Lingwood, Jonathan Buckley and Peter Anderson
Designer: Paul Calver and Louise Kirby
Illustrator: Liz Pepperall
Production Controller: Steve Lang

10 9 8 7 6 5 4 3 2 1

Some of the material in this book has been previously published as part of two larger books, *The Kitchen Garden Book* and *The World Encyclopedia of Fruit.*

Contents

Introduction

Berries and currants have always been one of the basic ingredients of our diet. Nowadays, we may have limited opportunities to gather wild berries from forests and often have to rely on supermarkets for supplies of cultivated soft fruits. However, by growing berries and currants for ourselves, we can still pick fresh, tasty fruits and eat them at the peak of their flavour, ripeness and goodness.

BERRIES FOR HEALTH

We are encouraged to eat fruit as part of a healthy, balanced diet and there is no doubt that fruit is good for us. All berries and currants are a good source of vitamin C, calcium, iron and fibre. Strawberries, raspberries and blackberries are an excellent source of phytochemicals which help protect against disease, and currants are a good source of vitamins A, B_1, B_2 and B_3.

Growing your own soft fruit means that you can ensure the fruits are grown without pesticides, and it won't be necessary to scrub the ripe fruits before you eat them. You also know what chemicals have been used. Fruit purchased from shops may have had a cocktail of chemicals sprayed on them as they grow so that they are offered to the consumer in pristine condition. In the garden, you can choose your own methods and use as few or as many chemicals as you like.

You can pick fruit as you need it and there should be enough berries to carry through from early summer right through to the frosts of late autumn or even early winter.

BERRIES FOR PLEASURE

Eating berries is not only good for you, but it is also a great pleasure. There are few greater delights than picking a luscious, ripe strawberry, still warm from the sun, and eating it on the spot. The same goes for raspberries and all the other berries.

Fruit bushes are also an attractive addition to the garden, especially when they are in flower, leaf and fruit, and some provide scent. They do not have to take up a lot of space and quite often canes can be trained against a wall, around posts or fences. Strawberries can easily be grown in a bed or border, along a path, or in containers. They can be ornamental, such as alpine strawberries, as well as fruit-bearing.

In addition to being eaten fresh, fruit plays a large part in cooking. A surprising number of sweet courses are based on, or include,

ABOVE Berries and currants are versatile fruits and can be used fresh or cooked in a wide variety of prepared dishes.

LEFT Picking fresh raspberries and eating them while still warm from the sun is one of life's small pleasures.

LEFT A mouthwatering selection of berries and currants fresh from the garden.

berries and currants. Many home-made ice creams and sorbets (sherbets) would be flavourless without them. They are also used in or with many savoury dishes and sauces, such as turkey with cranberry sauce. Jams and other delicious preserves depend on soft fruit in general, and berries, in particular, are the most popular.

Although it is second best, it is possible to utilize gluts of fruit by freezing or preserving them in other ways, such as bottling. They are worth having for cooking or serving with, for example, muesli and other breakfast cereals.

As well as a food, soft fruits have always been used in drinks of various kinds, from elderflower wine and blackcurrant cordial to simple fruit juices, such as cranberry. Many people are drinking fruit juices as an alternative to coffee and tea, as a healthy way of reducing their caffeine consumption.

GROWING YOUR OWN

There is no doubt that all fruit is best when it is eaten straight after being picked. It retains all its goodness and flavour. Shop-bought fruit bears no comparison to that grown in your own garden. You can choose cultivars that are worth growing for their flavour alone. Supermarkets and greengrocers are inclined to choose types that transport without bruising and those that have a long shelf-life. Flavour comes well down the list, even if it is considered at all.

One of the delights of growing a number of berries is the sheer range of flavours and textures. Admittedly, you cannot have fresh berries and currants all year round, you have to be content with each in its season, but most gardeners would settle for, say, a season of delicious strawberries rather than have indifferent berries from the supermarket all year round.

When planting your fruit bushes you should consider the type of soil in the garden, for example, raspberries will struggle in very alkaline soil with a pH higher than 6.5 and become iron-deficient with yellowing leaves. Blueberries and cranberries prefer acid soil preferably with pH 5.5 or less. Most soft fruits do well in rich loam-based soil that is free-draining but moisture-retentive.

Choosing the right site is important when planting fruit bushes. You should bear in mind the effects of frost and wind and provide suitable protection. You will also have to protect your fruit bushes from birds, squirrels and foxes and the best way is to install netting or use a fruit cage. To maintain healthy fruit crops, check the plants regularly for signs of pests and diseases, so that they can be dealt with quickly.

RIGHT Delicious strawberries can be grown in even the smallest of gardens.

Raspberries and cloudberries

Belonging to the rose family, raspberries are native to hilly areas of Europe and Asia, and grow best in a cool, damp climate. The deep red (sometimes yellow) fruits have a sweet, intense flavour, and many people prefer them to strawberries.

The fruits were not cultivated until the Middle Ages. Nowadays, in colder climates, they are cultivated from native European varieties, and in North America they derive from an indigenous species better suited to the generally, drier, hotter conditions there.

CULTIVARS

Wild raspberries – tiny, fragrant fruits – can often be found growing in cool, damp areas of woodland. They are full of pips, but their exquisite flavour makes up for this deficiency. Although there are many different cultivars available to gardeners and new ones are being developed all the time, the raspberries sold in shops and markets are only rarely identified. Gardeners often have their own favourites, however, and can also choose between summer- and autumn-fruiting types.

Among the best summer-fruiting raspberries are 'Glen Clova', which is an early-season cultivar, producing plentiful fruits, and 'Malling Jewel', which is another heavy cropper, fruiting in mid-season. Among the best autumn-fruiting raspberries are 'Heritage', which bears well-flavoured fruits, and 'Autumn Bliss', which bears masses of dark red fruits.

Yellow and gold-coloured raspberries are also available. 'All Gold', for example, is a prolific cropper, an autumn-fruiting variety that bears crumbly yellow fruits with a mild, sweet flavour that need careful handling.

Arctic raspberries are unusual but easy to grow and ornamental. The flavour is subtly different to normal raspberries. The plants only reach about 15–20cm/6–8in tall and die back during the winter.

CULTIVARS

Summer-fruiting

Early

'Delight'
'Glen Clova'
'Glen Coe'
'Glen Moy'
'Malling Exploit'
'Malling Promise'
'Sumner'

Mid-season

'Glen Lyon'
'Glen Prosen'
'Julia'
'Malling Jewel'
'Malling Orion'

Late

'Augusta'
'Leo'
'Malling Admiral'
'Malling Joy'

Autumn-fruiting

'All Gold'
'Autumn Bliss'
'Heritage'
'Norfolk Giant'
'September'

Raspberries

NUTRITION

Raspberries are a valuable source of phytochemicals, vitamin C, potassium, niacin and riboflavin, and dietary fibre. They contain 25 kilocalories per 100g/3¾oz. Raspberry juice is said to be good for the heart, while the leaves have long been renowned for their beneficial effects during childbirth; raspberry leaf tea is said to prevent miscarriages, ease labour and help the uterus to contract after the birth.

STORING

Raspberries are ripe when they are brightly and evenly coloured. When picked, they should slide easily off the hulls. If possible, always eat the berries the day they are picked; if necessary, they can be stored for up to two days in the bottom of the refrigerator, but bring them out at least an hour before serving.

Raspberries freeze well; whole berries emerge almost as good as before. Open freeze the fruit in a single layer on a baking sheet, then pack into rigid cartons. Less than perfect raspberries can be puréed and sieved, then sweetened with a little caster (superfine) sugar or icing (confectioner's) sugar before being frozen.

PREPARATION AND USE

Do not wash raspberries unless this is unavoidable; they are seldom very dirty, and washing will ruin the texture and flavour. Gently pick off any bits of leaf or stalk.

Good raspberries have such a wonderful flavour that they are best eaten on their own, with sugar and cream. They go well with other fruits, like oranges, apples, pears and melon. In the classic dish, Peach Melba, raspberries are used as a coulis to coat a lightly poached peach. They also make good fillings for pastries, pavlovas and tartlets, and, because they are so attractive, they are ideal for decoration.

Arctic raspberries

Raspberries can be crushed with icing sugar, then pushed through a nylon or stainless steel sieve to make sauces, coulis or bases for ice creams and sorbets (sherbets).

They can be cooked in pies; apple and raspberry is a classic combination. They are rich in pectin, so make excellent jams and jellies. Raspberry vinegar is delicious and makes delectable dressings and sauces.

CLOUDBERRIES

These deep golden relatives of the raspberry grow on boggy land in the cold northern climates of Scandinavia, Siberia and Canada, and even within the Arctic Circle.

Yellow raspberries

RASPBERRY COULIS

1 Put the wiped raspberries in a bowl and crush to a purée with a fork.

2 Tip the purée into a sieve set over a clean bowl. Rub through, using the back of a spoon.

3 Sweeten to taste with icing (confectioner's) sugar and stir.

Because they lack warmth, the berries ripen slowly, allowing the flavour to develop to an extra-ordinary intensity and sweetness, almost like honeyed apples. (Canadians call cloudberries "baked apple berries".) These unusual berries are highly prized in Scandinavian countries, where they are made into excellent jams, desserts and fruit soups.

The berries have an affinity with chocolate; try topping a chocolate mousse with a spoonful of cloudberry jam.

Blackberries and hybrid berries

Wild blackberries are closely related to raspberries, and a new range of delicious hybrid berries has been developed by crossing blackberries with raspberries or with another close relative, the dewberry. These tend to crop earlier than blackberries.

Archaeological excavations show that humans have eaten blackberries since Neolithic times. The ancient Greeks prized them as much for the medicinal properties of their leaves as for the fruit, but the fruit has always remained popular. Not everyone appreciates the qualities of wild brambles, however, and after early settlers introduced them to Australia they were declared a noxious weed in some areas.

CULTIVARS

The original blackberries, growing as brambles, are native to large parts of northern Europe and many Mediterranean countries. The shiny, purplish-black berries are made up of a number of segments, each containing a hard seed. Blackberries grow on vigorous, thorny, upright canes; dewberries, which are native to North America, grow on trailing, almost prostrate stems.

Over the years blackberries have been cultivated to give larger, juicier berries with better keeping properties than the wild fruit. There are also early- and late-fruiting plants and even some thornless types, such as the early-fruiting 'Merton Thornless' and the late-fruiting 'Oregon Thornless'.

FREEZING BLACKBERRIES

Blackberries freeze well. Open freeze perfect specimens in a single layer on a baking sheet, then pack into rigid containers. Damaged berries can be puréed and sieved, then sweetened with sugar or honey.

NUTRITION

Blackberries are an excellent source of phytochemicals and are rich in dietary fibre, iron and vitamin C, and they also contain some calcium, phosphorus and potassium. Being very juicy, they are often used to make health drinks and contain about 30 kilocalories per 100g/3¾oz. Loganberries contain twice as much vitamin C and twice as much citric acid as blackberries.

CULTIVARS

Blackberries

Early-fruiting
'Bedford Giant'
'Himalayan Giant'
'Merton Early'
'Merton Thornless'

Late-fruiting
'Ashton Cross'
'John Innes'
'Loch Ness'
'Oregon Thornless'
'Smoothstem'
'Thornfree'

Hybrid berries
Boysenberry
Loganberry
Marionberry
Sunberry
Tayberry
Tummelberry
Veitchberry
Youngberry

HYBRID BERRIES

Many hybrid berries have been produced over the years, some, such as the loganberry, arising as a natural cross, but others, such as the boysenberry, being cultivated to

Large blackberries

Wild blackberries or brambles

produce a more robust plant or better flavoured fruit. Hybrid berries tend to be less vigorous than blackberries, and they are, therefore, better suited to the small garden.

The first loganberry appeared in 1881 at Santa Cruz, California, in the garden of Judge J. H. Logan. It was a natural hybrid, probably derived from a cross between a native dewberry and a raspberry. Since then, loganberries have been hybridized to give large, juicy, dark wine-red berries that have the consistency of blackberries with an intense raspberry flavour. Clones include the thorned LY59 and the thornless L654. Loganberries are very tart and should be accompanied with plenty of sugar if they are eaten raw.

A hybrid between the dewberry and loganberry, youngberries resemble dark red, elongated blackberries, but they taste like sweeter loganberries.

Boysenberries, a cross between the youngberry and raspberry, bear fruits that resemble large, reddish-purple blackberries. Sweeter than loganberries, they can be eaten raw, and they are used to make jam.

Tayberries are widely regarded as the finest of all the hybrid berries. They were bred in Scotland as a cross between the American blackberry 'Aurora' and a tetraploid raspberry. They grow on long, spiny canes, and the bright red, elongated berries have a slightly tart, aromatic flavour. Although they can be eaten raw, they are better cooked.

Tummelberries are very similar to tayberries but bear fruit later in the season. The berries have a mild but sweet flavour. Similar hybrid berries include sunberries and the Japanese wineberry.

STORING

When you pick blackberries and other hybrid berries they should be plump and tender but not wet or mushy. Look for large, shiny fruits. According to legend, blackberries should not be picked after early autumn, or the Devil will be in them and they will taste sour, but the development of late-fruiting cultivars has effectively put paid to that superstition.

These berries do not keep well, and if you cannot eat them straight after picking, store them for no more than 24 hours in the bottom of the refrigerator.

PREPARATION AND USE

If you must wash these berries, do so just before serving and drain them thoroughly on kitchen paper.

Ripe, juicy blackberries are best eaten just as they are, with sugar and cream. They make a tasty addition to breakfast cereal or a fruit salad. They can also be puréed and sieved to make coulis, ice cream, sorbets (sherbets) and fools. They make delicious jam or bramble jelly and are the classic partner for apples in a pie or crumble. There is no need to cook them before using them as a pie filling or in a pudding. All these berries go well with many other fruits in addition to apples.

Tayberries

Blueberries and bilberries

Both blueberries and bilberries are small, round, blue-black fruits with a distinctive silvery bloom.

The bilberry, *Vaccinium myrtillus*, is found in Europe, Asia and North America, where it grows as a suckering shrub on acid, open heathland. The fruits, about 5mm/¼in across, are pale red, ripening to an intense blue-black in late summer and autumn.

Two types of blueberry, also species of *Vaccinium*, highbush and lowbush, are grown. Highbush blueberries, which are derived from the American wild blueberry, are very similar to bilberries, but the shrubs are larger and the berries are up to 1cm/½in across. Lowbush blueberries are low-growing shrubs, which produce smaller crops than the highbush types but are easier to grow.

CULTIVARS

Blueberries have been hybridized to give a range of cultivars that will bear fruit at different times, so that if several bushes are grown fruits will be available over a long period in summer to autumn. 'Jersey' is a vigorous plant, with sweet, well-flavoured berries. The vigorous 'Earliblue' is an early-cropping cultivar, with large clusters of light blue berries.

Bilberries, which are also known as blaeberries, whortle-berries or whinberries, are not grown commercially, although they may be available locally. There are no cultivated forms.

NUTRITION

Blueberries and bilberries are a good source of vitamin C, iron, dietary fibre and the phyto-chemicals that protect against disease. They provide about 60 kilocalories per 100g/3¾oz, with blueberries having a slightly higher sugar content than bilberries.

CULTIVARS

Blueberries

Early-fruiting
'Bluecrop'
'Bluetta'
'Earliblue'
'Patriot'

Mid-season
'Berkeley'
'Herbert'
'Ivanhoe'

Late-fruiting
'Coville'
'Darrow'
'Goldtraube 71'
'Jersey'

Blueberries

STORING FRUIT

If not eating immediately, freeze or preserve fruit by bottling or making into jam. Fruit can be kept for up to 12 months, depending on the method of preservation that has been used.

Bilberries

STORING

The best blueberries and bilberries for storing are plump, ripe berries of uniform size. Reject any shrivelled or damaged specimens and any without the characteristic silvery bloom. Unwashed berries will keep for up to a week in the bottom of the refrigerator. Blueberries and bilberries can be frozen just as they are provided they are in a sealed bag. Alternatively, poach them in a little lemon-flavoured syrup and then freeze.

PREPARATION AND USE

Both blueberries and bilberries contain soft seeds, so they can be eaten raw. Simply rinse and drain them first. They are, however, more usually baked in pies or muffins or used as a jam-like topping for a cheesecake. To cook this, you should make a light sugar syrup, flavour it with lemon, orange and cinnamon or allspice, and poach the berries in the syrup until they are tender. Dried blueberries are available in specialist food shops and make a tasty addition to fruit cakes and muesli.

BLUEBERRY RECIPES

Blueberry Pie (above) is a classic dessert, as is Blueberry Grunt, which consists of blueberries stewed with lemon and spice and baked with a dumpling-like topping. Blueberries can be made into a sauce to serve with game.

HUCKLEBERRIES

These tangy berries, which gave their name to Mark Twain's well-known character Huckleberry Finn, are native to North America, where they grow on an erect shrub, *Gaylussacia baccata*. The small, glossy black fruits are similar to blueberries but have a tougher skin and hard internal seeds. They have a much sharper flavour than blueberries, but they can still be eaten and cooked in exactly the same ways. The shrub should not be confused with the annual plant, known as garden huckleberry, *Solanum melanocerasum*, which also bears purple-black fruits.

The tangleberry is similar to the shrub huckleberry and it grows on the coasts of North America. The purplish-blue berries are a little sweeter than huckleberries and have a subtle tang of the sea.

Cranberries

These tart, bright red berries grow wild on evergreen shrubs in peaty marshland all over northern Europe and North America. They are closely related to blueberries and bilberries but are much more sour and are always served cooked. Cowberries and lingonberries are similar but smaller.

Cranberries are sometimes known as bounceberries, because they were traditionally tested for firmness by being bounced seven times. Any that failed the bounce test were too squashy and were discarded. Because of their waxy skins, cranberries keep for much longer than other berries, which helps to explain their popularity.

Do not confuse edible cranberries with American highbush cranberries (*Viburnum trilobum*) which are only for ornament or for wildlife.

For centuries before the first Europeans arrived in America, the native American Indians prized wild cranberries for their nutritional and medicinal value and used them to make a dye for fabric and for decorative feathers.

Although cranberries were known in Britain, the Pilgrim Fathers found that the American berries were larger and much more succulent. They called them craneberries because the pink blossoms resembled a crane's head, or possibly because the cranes, which lived in the marshlands, were partial to the berries. Cranberries featured in the first ever Thanksgiving feast in 1620 and have been a traditional part of the celebrations

CULTIVARS

'CN'
'Early Black'
'Franklin'
'Hamilton'
'McFarlin'
'Olson's Honkers'
'Pilgrim'

BELOW Dried cranberries, available from specialist stores, can be used in baked recipes with other dry ingredients.

RIGHT Bright red cranberries can be used in both sweet and savoury recipes.

ever since. Commercial cultivation began in the nineteenth century.

NUTRITION

Cranberries contain vitamins C and D, potassium and iron. They are considered to help prevent cystitis. They are naturally low in kilocalories but need sweetening to make them palatable.

STORING

Pick plump, firm, bright red berries. Fresh cranberries will keep in the refrigerator for four weeks, or they can be frozen in plastic bags and used without being thawed.

PREPARATION AND COOKING

Cranberries can be used in sweet or savoury dishes. Their most famous incarnation is as cranberry sauce, which is served with turkey or red meat and game. Their distinctive tartness even adds zest to firm-fleshed fish. The berries are high in pectin, so they make excellent jams and jellies. They combine well with orange and apple, and can be mixed with blackberries and raspberries to make an autumnal variation on summer pudding.

Cranberries should be stewed slowly with sugar to taste and a little water or orange juice until the skins pop. Dried cranberries can be used in the same way as raisins. Cranberry juice can be mixed with soda water and white wine or grape juice to make a refreshing drink. It is also good with orange juice and vodka.

CRANBERRY SAUCE

The traditional accompaniment for turkey at Christmas or Thanksgiving, cranberry sauce is made in advance and served cold.

1 Thinly pare an orange with a swivel-bladed vegetable peeler, taking care to remove only the zest. Squeeze the juice and put it in a pan with the zest.

2 Add 350g/12oz/3 cups cranberries and cook gently for a few minutes until the cranberry skins pop.

3 Stir in caster (superfine) sugar to taste and simmer for 5 minutes. Stir in 30ml/2 tbsp port (optional). Remove the zest, pour the sauce into a bowl, then cool and refrigerate before serving.

Gooseberries

The gooseberry, a botanical cousin of the redcurrant, is native to Europe and North America. The fruits, which grow on dauntingly spiny bushes, come in many varieties – hard and sour, succulently soft and sweet, smooth and hairy – and in a range of colours, from vivid green to luscious purple. They are deciduous bushes that tolerate a wide range of soils and last for years. They can also be grown as cordons, fans and standards.

Wild gooseberries were eaten in Britain for centuries and in the sixteenth century they began to be grown in kitchen gardens. The Tudors served them in savoury sauces and in many sweet dishes. By the nineteenth century they were so popular that competitors formed gooseberry clubs to see who could grow the biggest berry (some are reputed to have been grown to the size of a bantam's egg).

For some reason, their popularity did not spread abroad; even today the French use them only in a sauce to cut the richness of oily fish. There is no specific French word for gooseberry; it shares its name with the redcurrant and is only known as *groseille de maquereau* (literally translated as "redcurrant for mackerel").

CULTIVARS

Gooseberries have a very long season. Early fruits are usually bright green and hard, and they cannot be eaten raw, although they taste wonderful cooked. The softer, mid-season fruits follow these.

An early cultivar, 'Early Sulphur' has golden, almost translucent berries with a lovely sweet flavour. 'Golden Drop' is as attractive as its name. The small, round, yellow gooseberries have a fine, rich flavour, which make them ideal for eating raw as a dessert fruit.

'Invicta' bears white berries, usually used for cooking and is mildew resistant. 'Langley's Industry' bears large, red, hairy berries with a sweet flavour. It is an ideal gooseberry for the less green-fingered gardener because it will grow vigorously anywhere and can be picked in mid-season for cooking or left to ripen fully on the bush to eat raw.

'Leveller' is another mid-season cultivar, with yellowish-green berries with a sweet flavour. 'London', which is late-fruiting, has huge, deep red to purple berries, which can be eaten fresh, just as they are. Between 1829 and 1867 it was the unbeaten British champion in major gooseberry competitions.

CULTIVARS

Early-fruiting
'Broom Girl'
'Early Sulphur'
'Golden Drop'
'May Duke'

Mid-season
'Bedford Red'
'Careless'
'Greenfinch'
'Jubilee'
'Invicta'
'Langley's Industry'
'Whitesmith'

Late-fruiting
'Invicta'
'Lancashire Lad'
'Leveller'
'London'
'Whinham's Industry'
'White Lion'
'Yellow Champagne'

Green gooseberries

'London' red-fruited gooseberries

NUTRITION

Gooseberries are high in vitamin C and also contain vitamins A and D, potassium, calcium, phosphorus and niacin. They are rich in dietary fibre and provide only 17 kilocalories per 100g/3¾oz.

STORING

Choose slightly unripe green gooseberries for cooking. Check that they are not rock-hard. Dessert varieties should be soft and juicy (try to taste before you buy). They will keep in the refrigerator for up to a week. To freeze whole berries, top and tail them and open freeze on baking sheets. Pack the frozen berries into bags. Alternatively, purée and sieve them, sweeten and freeze in rigid containers.

PREPARATION AND USE

For recipes using whole gooseberries, wash, then top and tail them (this is not necessary if you are making jam or jelly, or are going to sieve or strain the cooked fruit).

Gooseberries are rich in pectin, particularly when they are slightly unripe, which makes them ideal for making jams, jellies and preserves. Their tartness makes an excellent foil for oily fish and rich poultry or meat. Cook gooseberries very gently with a little water and sugar to taste until all the fruit has collapsed. If you like, flavour them with cinnamon, lemon or herbs. A few dill or fennel seeds will enhance a gooseberry sauce for fish. Gooseberries also make a tasty filling for suet pudding or crumble. Puréed, sieved and mixed with whipped cream, they make the perfect fruit fool.

Gooseberries have an extraordinary affinity for elderflowers, which come into season at about the same time as the early fruit and add a delicious muscat flavour to the berries.

WORCESTERBERRIES AND JOSTABERRIES

The Worcesterberry is a form of a North American species of gooseberry. It grows as a bush armed with thorny spines, and the small, purple berries are not much larger than blackberries, but have the distinctive veining of gooseberries and tart, gooseberry flavour.

The Jostaberry is a hybrid of the gooseberry and blackcurrant. It is a vigorous shrub, rarely troubled by pests or diseases. The berries are similar to those of the Worcesterberry but are less freely borne.

TOPPING AND TAILING

Before gooseberries are eaten, the stalk and blossom end of the fruit must be removed. Hold the gooseberry between your forefinger and thumb and snip off the stem and flower end with sharp scissors or trim with a knife.

RIGHT Gooseberries are high in pectin and are ideal for making into jams and jellies, as are strawberries and blackberries.

Elderberries

These berries grow all over the countryside throughout the summer. The creamy-white flowerheads appear first and are followed by flat, wide clusters of small, almost black berries with a sweet, rich sickly taste.

Elderberries have grown in Europe and Asia since prehistoric times. The bushes themselves were little loved, perhaps because of their unattractive smell, but the berries provided sustenance for the poor. People often used elder-berries as a fabric dye and to make wine; later the berries were used to add colour and flavour to thin, cheap wines.

NUTRITION

Elderberries are an excellent source of vitamin C. In extract form, they contain antiviral agents which help prevent viruses penetrating cells.

CHOOSING AND STORING

Elderberries should be shiny and black. Never pick them close to a road, as they will be contaminated by pollution. For elderflower syrup choose creamy flowerheads that are fully open, but whose petals have not begun to drop. Neither berries nor flowers keep well.

Elderberries

PREPARATION AND COOKING

Use a fork to strip the berries off the stalks. Elderberries should be cooked as they are harmful when raw; cook them as for redcurrants or other berries. The flowers should be shaken to dislodge insects or loose petals and briefly rinsed in cold water.

The berries can be made into jellies or used with other berries in pies, tarts and fools. Elderberries are often used to make vinegar, and are excellent for making wine. Sprigs of elderflowers can be dipped in batter to make fritters.

Elderflowers can be made into a refreshing drink. To make eight 750ml/1¼ pint bottles, you will need about 12 large elderflower heads. Choose blossoms that are open, but not shedding their petals, and wash thoroughly. Place in a large pan and pour over 7 litres/12 pints boiling water. Add 250g/9oz caster (superfine) sugar, 2 sliced lemons and 120ml/4fl oz/½ cup white wine vinegar or cider vinegar. Stir and leave to macerate in a cool place for three days, stirring twice a day. Strain and pour into sterilized bottles. Cork firmly and leave for at least a week before drinking.

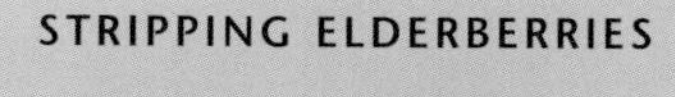

STRIPPING ELDERBERRIES

Hold the stalk in one hand and run a fork through the berries.

Elderflowers

Mulberries

These are handsome trees, which can achieve a great age. The white mulberry, *Morus alba*, is a spreading tree, to 10m/33ft tall and across, while the black mulberry, *Morus nigra*, has a more rounded crown and grows to 12m/40ft tall and to 15m/50ft across.

Black mulberries are believed to be native to southwest Asia. They were known to the ancient Greeks and Egyptians, but it was the Roman emperor, Justinian, who deliberately encouraged their propagation as part of an enterprise in silk production. In the sixteenth century Europeans discovered that the silkworms in China fed on mulberry leaves, and many trees were planted in Britain with the aim of producing silk. However, silkworms prefer white mulberry leaves; as the black ones were mistakenly planted, the silk project was a failure, but the trees were continued to be grown.

SPECIES

The black mulberry is the species grown for its edible berries. They are elongated, dark red fruits, resembling loganberries. They have a pleasant, if slightly acidic, flavour. White mulberries, which are pink or pale red, are edible but insipid. A North American species, *Morus rubra*, the red mulberry, bears sweet-tasting red fruits that ripen to purple.

NUTRITION

Black mulberries contain large amounts of potassium and vitamin C.

PREPARATION AND USE

Ripe mulberries can be eaten just as they are, with or without the addition of cream, and they are usually sweet enough not to need sugar. They are a good addition to summer pudding, and they can also be used in ice creams, fools and sorbets (sherbets). Over-ripe fruit is best used for jams, jellies and sauces. Mulberry sauce goes well with richly flavoured roasted meats, such as game, duck and lamb.

ARBUTUS

The arbutus or strawberry tree, *Arbutus unedo*, is a tall shrub or small tree, which produces edible, bright red fruits, which look somewhat like strawberries but have a different taste. The spiky, rather sweet berries have a soft, slightly mushy texture and a faint flavour of vanilla. The berries are not available in shops, but the trees are grown, usually for their ornamental value, in Europe as far north as western Ireland, where they are known as Killarney strawberries, and in the United States and China. Although they are unexciting to eat raw, the berries are sometimes used to make jellies and liqueurs.

Mulberries

planning and preparation

Growing soft fruit is not difficult, and there will be space in all but the smallest of gardens for a currant bush or two or for a few raspberry canes. When space is really limited, strawberries can be grown in containers on a sunny patio or balcony. As long as you prepare the ground thoroughly and look after your plants by feeding and pruning them when necessary you will be able to look forward to plentiful, delicious crops.

Types of soil

Soft fruits can, with a few exceptions, be grown on almost any type of soil, Strawberries are not very fussy and grow in most types, but will perform better in free-draining, slightly acidic, sandy loam-based soil with organic matter. Raspberries do not like alkaline soil and prefer fertile, free-draining with a pH of 6.5 or below.

CLAY

Usually high in fertility, which is a great advantage for growing most kinds of fruit, clay soils can be difficult to work. Clay is heavy, and the particles cling together, making the soil very sticky. Clay soil compacts easily, forming a solid lump that roots find hard to penetrate and that is difficult to dig. Try not to walk on clay soils when they are wet. This tendency to become compacted and sticky means that clay soils are slow to drain, but, once drained, they "set" like concrete, becoming a hard mass. They also tend to be cold and slow to warm up, making them unsuitable for early crops.

Because of the poor drainage and tendency to become waterlogged, clay soil can cause problems with many types of soft fruit. But, if the structure is improved, the moisture-retentiveness and fertility should enable you to produce excellent crops.

SANDY SOILS

Soils that are made up of sand and silts are quite different to clay soils. Sandy soils have few of the sticky clay particles but are made up of individual grains that allow the water to pass through quickly. This quick passage of water through the soil tends to leach (wash) out nutrients, so the soils are often poor. But they also tend to be much warmer in winter and are quicker to warm up in spring, thus making it easier to get early crops. Silts contain particles that are more clay-like in texture than those found in sandy soils, and they hold more moisture and nutrients.

Both types of soil are easy to improve and are not difficult to work. Sand does not compact as clay does, but silty soils are more susceptible to the impact of feet and wheelbarrows. Adding plenty of well-rotted organic material can temper their insatiable thirst.

pH VALUES

1.0	extremely acid
4.0	maximum acidity tolerated by most plants
5.5	maximum acidity for reasonable fruit
6.0	maximum acidity for good fruit
6.5	optimum for the best fruit
7.0	neutral, maximum alkalinity for reasonable fruit
7.5	maximum alkalinity for most fruit
8.0	maximum tolerated by most plants
14.0	extremely alkaline

LOAMS

The soil of most gardeners' dreams is loam. This is a combination of clay and sandy soils, with the best elements of both. Loam tends to be free-draining, but at the same time moisture-retentive. This description – free-draining and moisture-retentive – is often used of soils and potting mixes, and it may seem to be a contradiction. It means that the soil is sufficiently free-draining to allow excess moisture to drain away, so that plants do not stand in stagnant water.

Such soils are extremely easy to work at any time, and they warm up well in spring and are excellent for producing early crops.

COMMON TYPES OF SOIL

SAND
Free-draining and quick to warm up, but hungry and thirsty.

LOAM
More moisture-retentive, warms quickly and works perfectly.

SILT
River deposits can be sticky, but not as sticky as clay. Easy to work.

CLAY
Heavy and often difficult to work. Slow to warm up, but fairly rich.

TESTING THE SOIL FOR NUTRIENTS

1 Collect the soil sample 5–8cm/2–3in below the surface. Take a number of samples, and test each one separately.

2 With this kit, mix one part of soil with five parts of water. Shake well in a jar, then allow the water to settle.

3 Draw off some of the settled liquid from the top few centimetres (about an inch) for your test.

4 Carefully transfer the solution to the test chamber in the plastic container, using the pipette.

5 Select a colour-coded capsule (one for each nutrient). Put the powder in the chamber, replace the cap and shake.

6 After a few minutes, compare the colour of the liquid with the shade panel of the container.

ACID AND ALKALINE SOILS

Another way of classifying soils is by their acidity or alkalinity. Those that are based on peat (peat moss) are acid; those that include chalk or limestone are alkaline. A scale of pH levels is used (not just by gardeners) to indicate the degree of acidity or alkalinity. Very acid is 1, neutral is 7 and very alkaline is 14, although soils rarely have values at the extremes of the scale. Although they can be grown on a wide range of soils, most soft fruits are grown on soils with a pH of 5.5–7, with the optimum conditions being around 6.5. However, bilberries, blueberries and cranberries require very acid soil. You can test your garden with a soil testing kit. It is quite easy to make an acid soil alkaline, but more difficult to make an alkaline more acid.

IMPROVING HEAVY SOIL

If soil is very waterlogged, you may need to dig drainage channels, but in most cases improving the soil structure is all that is needed. One way to achieve this is to add organic material. The fibrous material contained in the organic matter helps to break up the clay particles, allowing water to pass through. This material eventually breaks down and so it should be added every time the soil is dug.

The other method is to add gravel or grit to the soil. The best material for this is known as horticultural grit – that is, sharp grit up to about 5mm/¼in in diameter. Flint grit that has been crushed is best because the angular faces allow water to drain away more quickly than the rounded surfaces of the uncrushed grits, such as peabeach.

Soil improvement

Perhaps the most important task in any garden is to improve and maintain the quality of the soil. Good quality soil should be the aim of any gardener who wants to grow soft fruits, and to ignore the soil is to ignore one of the garden's most important assets.

ORGANIC MATERIAL

The key to improving the soil in your garden is organic material, a term that covers any vegetable matter that has been broken down into an odourless, fibrous compost. It includes such things as rotted garden waste, kitchen vegetable waste, farmyard manures and other plant waste material.

It is important that any such material should be well-rotted. If it is still in the process of breaking down, it will need nitrogen to complete the process and will extract it from the soil. This, of course, is the reverse of what the gardener wants – the gardener's aim is, in fact, to add nitrogen to the soil. If you are unsure, a good indicator that the material has broken down sufficiently is that it becomes odourless. Even horse manure is free from odour once it has rotted down.

Some substances contain undesirable chemicals, but these will be removed if the material is allowed to weather. Bark and other shredded woody materials may contain resins, for example, while animal and bird manures may contain ammonia. These chemicals will eventually evaporate or be converted by weathering.

ABOVE Green manure helps to improve both the structure and fertility of the soil. Sow it when the ground is not being used for anything else and then dig it in before it flowers and sets seed.

DIGGING IN

The best way to apply organic material to the fruit garden is to dig it in and incorporate it into the soil. If possible, double dig the bed, adding material all the way to the bottom of both spits. This will help to retain moisture and supply nutrients where they are needed, which is near the roots. It will also encourage roots to delve deeply rather than remaining on the surface, where easy water can be obtained from the odd rain shower or watering can. The deeper the roots go the more stable will be the plant's water supply and it will grow at a regular pace rather than in fits and starts.

TOP-DRESSING

Once the ground has been planted, especially with permanent fruit, it is impossible to dig in organic material any further than just below

ABOVE Soil that has been dug in the autumn can have more organic matter worked into the top layer of the soil in the spring. Spread the organic matter over the surface.

LEFT The acidity of the soil can be reduced by adding lime some weeks before planting and working it in with a rake. Check the soil with a soil testing kit to see how much lime is required.

the surface. The damage done by disturbing roots makes it pointless to attempt to dig deeply. Instead, top-dress with well-rotted matter. A 10cm/4in layer of, say, farmyard manure will be slowly worked into the soil by the earthworms. As well as being taken into the soil, such a dressing will also act as a mulch, protecting the ground from drying out as well as preventing any weed seeds from germinating.

The top-dressing should also be free from any weed seeds. Properly made compost and the other types of material that can be used should always be weed-free and suitable for use in this way.

IMPROVING THE SOIL'S pH

Another aspect of improving soil is to improve the pH level. For most soft fruits a soil pH of 6.5–7 is acceptable. Raspberries, however, cannot take up iron if the pH is above 6.5. Blueberries and cranberries need a pH of 5.5 or lower.

If the soil is too acid, the pH can be adjusted somewhat by adding lime. Ordinary lime (calcium carbonate) is the safest to use. Quicklime (calcium oxide) is the strongest and most caustic, but it may cause damage. Slaked lime (calcium hydroxide) is quicklime with water added; it is not as strong as quicklime and is therefore less dangerous. Always wear gloves and take safety precautions when you are applying lime and follow the quantities recommended by the manufacturer on the packet. Do not add lime at the same time as manure, because this will release ammonia, which can damage the plants. Spread the lime over the soil at the rate prescribed on the packet and rake it in. Alternately, add dolomitic lime.

It is not as easy to reduce the alkalinity of soil. Peat (peat moss) used to be recommended for this purpose, but not only is collecting peat environmentally unsound, it breaks down quickly and needs to be constantly replaced. Most organic manures are on the acid side and help to bring down the levels. Leaf mould, especially that from pine trees, is also acid.

Spent mushroom compost contains lime and thus will reduce acidity, so it is best not used on chalky (alkaline) soils.

ABOVE It is best to avoid working on wet soil, but sometimes it is necessary. To ensure that the soil is not compacted and its structure destroyed, it is advisable to work from a plank of wood.

IMPROVING SOIL STRUCTURE

1 One of the best ways to improve the structure of the soil is to add as much organic material as you can, preferably when the soil is dug. For heavy soils, this is best done in the autumn.

2 If the soil has already been dug, well-rotted organic material can be worked into the surface of the soil with a fork. The worms will complete the task of working it into the soil.

Growing soft fruit

In terms of harvest per square metre/yard, growing fruit can be much more economical than vegetables, and although buying canes and bushes will be more expensive than seeds, they will last for many years and repay the initial outlay many times over. This is something to bear in mind when you are planning what crops to grow.

CHOOSING A SITE

All fruit will do better if it is grown in full sun, so when you are planning a fruit garden take care that you avoid areas of the garden that are in the deep shade cast by large trees. The trees will, in any case, compete with the canes and bushes for nutrients. Most soft fruit will grow and crop well in a light shade or if it is growing where it is in shade for part of the day.

Ideally, you should choose a position where the fruit will not be buffeted by strong winds, which can affect pollination, cause slow or distorted growth and may lead to premature blossom or fruit drop. Fruit canes subjected to wind-rock are more susceptible to pests and diseases. If necessary, erect windbreaks, in the form of low hedges or a screen.

Where possible, plant fruit where there is no danger that it will be in a frost pocket, which sometimes occurs when the garden slopes down and ends in a solid barrier, such as a fence or wall. Cold air will accumulate in this area and will be unable to pass through the barrier. Replacing the fence with a hedge will allow the cold air to dissipate and flow freely away.

CHOOSING FRUIT

As long as it will grow in your garden there is nothing to prevent you from choosing any fruit you want to grow. Bear in mind, however, that blueberries and cranberries need acid soil, so do not consider growing these if your soil is very alkaline; you will struggle to give them the conditions they want. Raspberries, too, need soil that is on the acid side of neutral, so again, if your garden soil is very alkaline or has been recently limed, avoid raspberries.

Extend the season over which you can harvest fruits by choosing cultivars that crop at different times. Raspberries and gooseberries, for example, have been bred to produce early-, mid-season and late-fruiting cultivars, and even if

LEFT Strawberries can be grown in containers under glass, as here, and an early crop can be obtained.

ABOVE In the autumn, and again in the spring, top-dress fruit bushes with a layer of well-rotted organic material such as farmyard manure.

ABOVE Strawberries can be grown through a black plastic mulch. This not only protects the fruit from mud splashes, but also reduces the need for weeding and watering.

you do not choose different named cultivars, consider planting one bush in a shadier part of the garden than another so that the plant that receives more sun crops earlier than the one in shade.

PLANTING

Before planting, prepare the ground thoroughly. Double digging and even single digging are no longer regarded as essential, but before planting something new it is worth digging over the plot to remove all debris and perennial weed roots. Take the opportunity to dig in plenty of well-rotted manure. In subsequent years, regular mulching will gradually improve the quality of the soil and you will not disturb the soil's underlying structure or bring weed seeds to the surface where they will immediately germinate.

As long as the weather is neither too wet nor too cold the best time to plant new bushes and canes is between late autumn and mid-spring. If you have bought bare-rooted plants and they are delivered when you cannot plant them, heel them in (leaning over, almost horizontal) in a spare piece of ground. Container-grown plants can be planted at any time of the year as long as the ground is not waterlogged or frozen, although they are likely to need more attention, especially watering, if they are planted in summer.

When you plant the bush or canes, water them in well and apply a mulch about 5cm/2in deep to help conserve the moisture in the ground and to suppress weeds, which will compete with the plants for nutrients and moisture.

CONTAINERS

Although cane fruit (raspberries, blackberries and hybrid berries) should be grown in the open garden, there is no reason why shrubs and bushes cannot be grown in a container. Choose the largest possible container you can and use good quality compost (soil mix). Because the plants will be in the containers for a long time, replace the top layer of compost each spring, without damaging the roots. Always site containers where they can be easily watered.

Strawberries are ideal to grow in containers. They will grow in anything from small, individual pots or strawberry pots, to growing bags or special towers, which keep the fruits off the ground. All these are available from garden centres or nurseries. Because they are greedy feeders, do not use the compost from a used growing bag for anything else. Add it to the compost heap or, if the strawberries were completely unaffected by pests and diseases, use it as a mulch in the ornamental garden.

Supporting canes and shrubs

Once they are established, currant bushes can be grown as free-standing plants that will need little in the way of protection and support. It is, however, possible to train gooseberries and red- and whitecurrants as cordons or fans, and cane fruit needs to be grown against a framework of wires to which the individual canes are tied.

WALL-TRAINED PLANTS

When fruit bushes are grown as cordons or fans against a wall they can look very decorative. In addition, they often benefit from the protection afforded by the wall and produce better crops. It is important that they are tied into a secure frame-work, and this usually takes the form of parallel wires.

So that the supports last for as long as possible, use galvanized fencing wire, which will not corrode and will be strong enough to bear the weight of the full-grown plant. The wire should be held in place with galvanized nails or with vine eyes, of which there are several types available. Some are flat, metal spikes, which are hammered into the brickwork. Others are screw eyes, which are screwed into wall plugs that have been inserted into holes in the brick or stonework of the wall. This type can be screwed directly into wooden fences. Use straining bolts at one end to make it easier to keep the wire taut. If you prefer, wire mesh or wooden trellis can be fixed to the wall and used to support the plant.

Vine eyes should be positioned about 60–90cm/2–3ft apart to make sure that the wires are securely held. The wires should be placed so that they coincide with the horizontal branches of the plant, but it is usually sufficient to arrange them so that they are 30–45cm/ 12–18in apart, with the lowest wire 45–60cm/18–24in from the base of the wall and the top wire about 15cm/6in below the top of the wall.

So that air can circulate freely around the plant and to make it easier to prune plants and to harvest the fruit, make sure that the wires, trellis or mesh are held 5–8cm/2–3in away from the wall. The easiest way to do this is to attach wooden blocks or posts to the wall and to screw the vine eyes to the blocks. If you use trellis, use hinges along the lower edges and simply hook the top of the trellis to wooden blocks so that you can lower the trellis if necessary. This is useful if you need to paint or repair the wall behind the plant.

When you plant a bush against a wall, dig the hole about 45cm/ 18in away from the foot of the wall and put plenty of moisture-retentive humus in the bottom of the hole. Walls cast 'rain shadows', and the soil in the lee of a wall or fence is often quite dry. Positioning the plant a short distance from the wall will help to make sure that its roots get plenty of rainwater so that you do not have to water it continually. Until the plant reaches the wire or

ERECTING WIRES FOR WALL-TRAINED PLANTS

1 To support shrubs against a wall use wires held by vine eyes. Depending on the type of vine eye, either knock them into the wall or drill and plug before screwing them in.

2 Thread galvanized wire through the holes in the vine eyes and fasten to the end ones, keeping the wire as taut as possible.

1 Knock a stout post well into the ground at the end of the row. Alternatively, dig a hole and insert the post before refilling and ramming down the earth.

2 Knock another post at a 45° angle to the vertical to act as a support for the upright post. Nail it firmly so that the upright post is rigid and will not be pulled by tight wires.

3 Fasten the wire around one end post and pull tight, stapling it to each post. Keep the wire as taut as possible. If necessary, use eye-bolts on the end posts so that you can tension the wire.

4 Fasten the canes, in this case raspberry canes, to the wire with string or plant ties. Space the canes out evenly so that the maximum amount of light reaches the leaves and fruit.

trellis, guide it towards the wall by tying it to a bamboo cane placed at an angle, which can be removed when the plant reaches its supports.

SUPPORTING CANE FRUIT

Raspberries, blackberries and the various hybrid berries need a permanent framework of posts and wires. These plants are grown in the open, and the support must be put in position before the canes are planted. If you have space, arrange the wire framework so that it runs north–south so that the plants do not shade each other too much.

The end posts are the most important part of the structure because they take a strain in one direction only, and if they are not secured properly they can be pulled from the ground. Each post should be of tanalized (pressure-treated) wood so that it will not rot in the ground or need replacing. Each end post should be sunk into the ground by at least 60cm/24in and braced with another post, set at an angle to it. Intermediate posts, set about 2m/6ft apart, should be set to a similar depth but do not need bracing.

Parallel lengths of galvanized wire are stretched along the length of the row at intervals of 30cm/12in with the lowest wire about 60cm/24in from the ground. These wires should be as taut as possible. Fix them with staples, or holes can be drilled in the posts and eye-bolts inserted, which can be used to tension the wire by tightening the nut on the outside of the end posts.

Protecting fruit

Gardeners are not the only animals to like fruit. Many others, birds in particular, do so as well, and the only way to make sure that there is enough left for the gardener to enjoy is to protect fruit bushes. The most practicable way is to put a physical barrier between the predators and the fruit.

FRUIT CAGES

The easiest way to protect fruit is with a cage. The advantages are that it covers the area completely and the gardener can walk around within it to maintain the bushes or harvest the fruit. When individual protection is provided each cover has to be removed in turn, which can be tiresome, especially if netting snags on branches.

Ready-made fruit cages are expensive but are probably cheaper than making one of your own, unless you have access to free materials. Fruit cages are supplied in kit form and are easy to erect; they can usually be ordered to whatever size you require. Make sure that there are no gaps in the netting and that it is well pegged down or buried at the base because birds have a knack of finding the smallest hole to squeeze through.

Making a fruit cage is time-consuming, but you can make it fit any shape and cover any area you want. Metal posts, such as scaffolding poles, will last for ever but most gardeners find that wooden poles are more practical. They should be sturdy and treated with preservative. Each should be set into the ground by about 60cm/24in for security, because the netting will act as a sail, putting great pressure on the posts in strong winds.

ABOVE A tunnel of wire netting can be used to protect low-growing strawberries. The netting can be in short sections for easy removal and storage.

The covering can be plastic netting, but galvanized wire netting will last longer and be less likely to tear accidentally. Some gardeners like to remove the top covering to allow birds in to eat pests when the fruit is not actually ripening, and if you want to do this, use wire sides and a plastic netting for the top. Another reason for being able to remove the top covering in winter, especially if it is plastic, is that a heavy fall of snow can stretch and break it. The tops of the poles are best covered with a smooth rounded object – the bottom of a plastic drinks bottle is ideal – and although it may look ugly, it will prevent the plastic netting from being chafed and worn as the wind moves it against the posts.

Make a door wide enough to get a wheelbarrow through and make certain that it fits well, or

LEFT A fruit cage is expensive but is the most effective way of protecting fruit from birds.

birds will get in. Open the cage when plants are in flower so that pollinating insects can enter.

LOW-LEVEL PROTECTION

It is easier to provide protection for individual crops when low-level protection is required because less material is needed. Simply bend some wire netting into an inverted U-shape and peg it to the ground with wires. This works well for strawberries. Alternatively, put short stakes in the ground at intervals all round and in the middle of the crop and drape plastic netting over them.

DRAPED NETTING

There is no satisfactory way of protecting taller, free-growing subjects, such as fruit bushes or trees. Draping them with netting is the only possible method, but gaps are usually left and the netting snags on twigs and shoots.

If a fruit bush is growing against a wall or fence, then the netting can be held away from the plant by building a simple frame, and this can also be covered with plastic in spring to protect the blossom against frost.

NON-NETTING PROTECTION

Netting is the only satisfactory way to protect fruit crops in the garden. Commercial methods, such as bangers, are impracticable in a domestic garden. Humming wires have limited success but do not really work. Covering the bushes with black cotton threads may keep the birds off but make harvesting awkward and they are difficult to remove for pruning.

LEFT Strawberries can be protected against frost with cloches.

ABOVE Fruit trees and bushes trained against a wall or fence can be protected with a home-made frame. The frame can also be covered with plastic to protect the blossom from frosts.

The traditional scarecrow makes a good feature in the garden, but it has no success in deterring birds and animals. In fact, birds will often use the arms as perches before grabbing the fruit. Plastic birds of prey or owls at strategic points often work well for a while, but birds soon get used to them.

Propagation

While most gardeners do not have much space to increase their stock, and many do not need to replace their tree fruit, they need to know how to propagate soft fruits, so that they can be replaced from time to time. The propagation techniques are all fairly simple to master.

HARDWOOD CUTTINGS

Currants, gooseberries and blueberries (in warmer climates) are usually increased by taking hardwood cuttings. This process does not need any propagators or equipment other than a pair of secateurs (pruners) or a sharp knife.

The best time for taking hardwood cuttings is autumn, preferably early autumn. Select a few shoots that have grown during the previous year and are now firm and well ripened. They should be straight and about 30cm/12in long.

Choose a sheltered site, away from drying winds and hot sun. Make a narrow trench by inserting a spade into the soil and pushing it to one side to open up a narrow, V-shaped slit. If the soil is heavy, trickle some clean sharp sand into the bottom of the slit and insert the cuttings. Place them about 15cm/6in apart, planting them so that about half of the cutting is below ground. Place the spade into the ground about 10cm/4in away from the initial slit and lever it so that the slit closes up, firmly holding the cuttings. Firm down the soil gently with your feet.

By the next autumn the cuttings should have rooted. They can be dug up and transplanted to their final positions or moved to a nursery bed for another year.

LAYERING

Blackberries and hybrid berries are best increased by the simple process of layering, as are strawberries, which are usually obliging enough to do it themselves, by sending out runners, leaving the gardener to transplant the new plants.

During the growing season, choose a healthy blackberry cane that is long enough to touch the ground. Where the tip makes contact with the soil, dig a hole about 10cm/4in deep. Place the tip

METHODS OF PROPAGATION

Division: Blackberries, hybrid berries, raspberries and strawberries

Layering: Blackberries, hybrid berries and strawberries

Hardwood cuttings: Blackcurrants, gooseberries, redcurrants and whitecurrants

Semi-ripe cuttings: Blueberries

Tip rooting: Blackberries and hybrid berries

LAYERING

1 Blackberries, hybrid berries and strawberries can be increased by layering. Bend over a healthy shoot, dig a hole near the tip and then bury it.

2 After a short period the tip will have produced roots. It can then be cut from the parent plant and replanted where required.

3 If you would like to have ready-potted specimens, bury a pot in the ground, fill it with compost (soil mix) and bury the tip in this.

1 Take hardwood cuttings in autumn, with each cutting about 30cm/12in in length. Cut just below a bud.

2 Push a spade into the ground and lever it backwards and forwards. If the ground is heavy, part fill the slit with some clean sharp sand.

3 Place the hardwood cuttings vertically into the trench at about 15cm/6in intervals.

in it and bury it by replacing the soil. If you wish, secure it with a peg, although this is not normally necessary. By late autumn the tip will have rooted. Cut the new plant from its parent shoot, about 30cm/12in from the ground, and transplant it to its fruiting position.

It is possible to bury the tip of the parent cane into a pot of potting compost (soil mix) instead of a hole in the ground; it will root just as easily. The pot can be sunk into the ground, which will prevent it from being knocked over and it will not dry out as quickly as it would if left standing on the ground.

Strawberries can be treated in a similar way. After fruiting they send out runners, which will drop roots at intervals along their length to produce new plants. You can peg them down or cover a short length of runner with soil, but this is usually unnecessary as the plant will root itself quite naturally.

4 Dig the spade in a short distance from the trench and lever it so that the slit closes up.

5 Firm down the soil around the cuttings with your foot and generally tidy up the surface of the soil with a rake.

Again, the runners can be pegged into pots of compost if you want ready-potted plants.

DIVISION

Raspberries are usually increased by division. It is a simple matter to lift some of the suckers that emerge a little way from the parent plant. In autumn dig up a healthy, strong-growing sucker and cut through the root that is still attached to the main clump. Replant this in its fruiting position. It is advisable never to divide diseased plants for replanting. If you are in any doubt, it is always better to start from scratch, using certified disease-free stock that has been sold by a reputable nursery.

Common pests

Organic gardeners, who work hard to encourage birds into their gardens to keep down insect pests, find that not only do they have to protect soft fruit from birds but also act to counter pests that the birds would otherwise keep down. The advice given here should help you decide on what level you choose to use chemicals in the garden and help you garden organically if you wish.

APHIDS

Greenfly and blackfly suck sap from leaves and young shoots and cause leaf curl, stunted growth and sooty mould. They also transmit viral diseases.

Spray cane and bush fruit (not strawberries) with tar oil wash in winter to kill overwintering eggs. If aphids continue to be a problem spray with a systemic insecticide (such as pirimicarb, dimethoate or heptenophos) in spring, repeating the treatment as directed on the package. Organic gardeners should spray with insecticidal soap and encourage predators, such as ladybirds (ladybugs), hoverflies and ground beetles. The tips of blackcurrants can be dipped into a bucket containing a solution of soft soap.

BIG BUD MITE

Blackcurrants may be infested by microscopic mites, which live inside the developing buds, making them rounded and swollen. Reversion, a viral disease, is spread by the mites.

In winter pick off and burn the big, rounded buds (uninfected buds are narrow and pointed); badly infested plants should be dug up and burned.

CAPSID BUGS

Currants and gooseberries may be infested by the bugs, which suck sap from shoots, leaves and fruits.

Spray with pirimiphos-methyl, fenitrothion or dimethoate when the flowers have fallen.

ABOVE Aphids, such as blackfly, will colonize young, tender growth. Check the undersides of leaves.

EELWORMS

Deformed and discoloured strawberry leaves may indicate the presence of eelworms, microscopic organisms that tunnel through plant tissue. There is no cure and infected plants should be burned.

RASPBERRY BEETLE

In late spring the beetles begin to feed on the blossom not only of raspberries but also of loganberries and blackberries. The yellow-brown larvae tunnel into developing fruits, which often become shrivelled, but it may not be noticed until the fruits are picked. As flowering ends spray with fenitrothion, derris or malathion. Hoe around canes in winter to expose the overwintering pupae to birds and remove any mulch, replacing it with new material in spring.

LEFT Biological controls are a good way to fight pests. The control insects are released to attack the pests.

RASPBERRY CANE MIDGE

Adult midges emerge from the soil in spring and early summer and lay eggs in cracks in canes. When the larvae hatch out, they feed on the plant tissue for a month, and cane blight often invades the infected canes, leading to dieback.

Hoe around the canes in winter to expose the pupae to birds and spray the base of the canes with derris or carbendazim in spring.

RED SPIDER MITE

Although this is most often found in the greenhouse, strawberries, raspberries and currants can be infested in hot weather, and plants growing close to a fence or wall are particularly susceptible because the air may be stagnant.

Spray with heptenophos and permethrin or with pirimiphos-methyl. Use insecticidal soap. Prevent infestations by keeping plants growing strongly, in moisture-retentive soil. After harvesting the fruit, cut off all leaves and clear away and burn any debris.

REDCURRANT BLISTER APHIDS

Green or red blisters appear on the leaves, and aphids may be visible under the leaves. In winter spray with tar oil wash to kill overwintering eggs; repeat after two weeks. Spray again in autumn, after leaf-fall. Rake up and burn all fallen leaves.

SAWFLY

The gooseberry sawfly caterpillar, about 1.5–3cm/½–1¾in long, which is green with black spots, can strip the leaves from bushes but will be killed by derris, fenitrothion, malathion or pyrethrum. Or you can pick off the caterpillars by hand or put some newspaper under the bushes and shake them vigorously. The caterpillars will drop off and can be killed.

SLUGS AND SNAILS

These pests can do enormous damage to fruit crops. To prevent them, cultivate the land to expose the eggs to predators and encourage predators like frogs. Alternatively, sink saucers of beer in the ground to drown them or go out at night with a torch (flashlight) and collect them. Strew surplus seedlings, leaves or bran around young plants so that the slugs and snails will be attracted to these and not the crops. You can spray with liquid metaldehyde or a product based on aluminium sulphate or scatter slug pellets around, but these can harm wildlife and pets.

ABOVE Slugs and snails have few friends among gardeners. They make holes in just about any part of a plant, often leaving it useless or even dead.

Always check the manufacturer's instructions regarding the timing of harvesting after using pellets.

STRAWBERRY BEETLE

In early summer these black ground beetles, about 2cm/¾in long, eat pieces of fruit, causing damage that is similar to that caused by birds. Remove all debris and dead leaves. Methiocarb slug pellets can be used, but check when it is safe to harvest on the manufacturer's packaging.

RIGHT Red spider mites produce a distinctive webbing of fine white silk.

Common diseases and disorders

Good housekeeping can prevent many diseases. Remove all diseased and rotting material as soon as you notice it, and plant material that is infected with viral diseases should be burned. Although it may seem wasteful to burn fruit, it is better to safeguard healthy plants and to prevent spores from getting into the soil, from where they will infect the following year's crops.

ARABIS MOSAIC VIRUS

Strawberry leaves become mottled and plants are distorted. The virus is transmitted by eelworms, and there is no chemical control. Lift and burn infected plants.

BOTRYTIS

This fungal problem, often called grey mould, is particularly common in cold, damp conditions. It affects strawberries, when both leaves and fruit may be covered with a greyish, velvety fungus, but cane fruits and currants are also susceptible.

Spray with carbendazim when flowers appear. If possible, burn infected plants; otherwise, pick off all infected leaves and overripe fruit and improve the ventilation. Water in the morning, not in the evening, to reduce humidity.

CANE BLIGHT

The leaves on fruiting raspberry canes wilt and wither in summer, and in strong wind the canes may just snap. Dark patches on the canes can usually be seen at ground level, and the bark often splits and cracks.

Cut out all diseased canes below ground level and burn them. Disinfect your knife or secateurs. Spray new canes with Bordeaux mixture. Make sure that canes are securely tied to the wires to prevent wind-rock in winter, so that the canes will be more resilient.

CANE SPOT

This bacterial problem causes purplish, round spots on the canes of hybrid berries, raspberries and occasionally blackberries. Cankers may develop on the spots, leaves have white-centred spots, and the fruits are misshapen.

To treat this, cut out and burn any affected fruit canes. Spray with carbendazim every two weeks from bud burst until the end of the flowering season.

LEFT The leaves on this raspberry bush are withering, which is often a sign of cane blight. Affected canes should be destroyed.

CHLOROSIS

Fruits growing on chalky, alkaline soil, especially raspberries, may have yellow or white bands between the veins of the leaves. Dig in plenty of humus at planting time and reduce the alkalinity of the soil by applying chelated compound or fritted trace elements.

CORAL SPOT

Redcurrant bushes (occasionally other currants) sometimes have pink or reddish spots on dead twigs. If this fungal problem spreads to healthy shoots it may kill the bush, especially if it has recently been stressed (perhaps by transplanting, drought or waterlogging).

Cut out and burn all affected shoots at least 10cm/4in below the area that appears diseased. Remove and burn all the plant debris from around the bushes.

CRINKLE

This virus, which can affect strawberries, is transmitted by aphids. The leaves have yellow spots, with red or purplish centres. In a severe infection the spots spread and turn brown and the leaves pucker. Burn diseased plants and take steps to control aphids.

CROWN GALL

Walnut-sized galls can be seen at ground level near cane fruits or small chains of galls develop higher up on the canes. Remove and burn diseased canes.

RIGHT Mildew covers leaves with a fine, whitish-grey powder.

LEAF SPOT

This problem, especially common in wet summers, affects many plants, especially blackcurrants and gooseberries, and sometimes causes entire leaves to turn brown. Plants lose vigour as leaves shrivel and drop. Remove and burn diseased leaves and spray the plants with Bordeaux mixture, mancozeb or carbendazim.

LEAFY GALL

This bacterial disease sometimes causes strawberries to produce abortive shoots that are flattened and that bear distorted leaves at soil level. Remove and burn all infected plants and sterilize your tools.

MAGNESIUM DEFICIENCY

Raspberries may develop orange, red or brown bands between the veins of the leaves. Spray with magnesium sulphate and repeat after two weeks.

MILDEW

Both downy and powdery mildew, which cause whitish-grey fungal growths on leaves, flowers and shoots, are a problem in humid, overcrowded conditions. Remove and burn affected leaves and spray plants with Bordeaux mixture. Water well and make sure that all bushes and canes are well mulched.

European gooseberry mildew (which also affects blackcurrants and, sometimes, redcurrants) causes a white powdery covering on the upper surface of the leaves, and it may spread to the underside and to the berries. Old bushes are very susceptible. Do not overcrowd bushes and keep weeds under control. Prune to keep bushes open so that air and light can get to all parts of the plant.

The more serious American gooseberry mildew causes powdery white fungal growths on leaves, shoots and fruit. Eventually, the patches become brown and felty. Shoots may be distorted, and fruits are small and tasteless. Cut out and burn infected shoots and spray with carbendazim or with bupirimate and triforine. The disease is worse in humid weather and when the soil is dry, so mulch plants and make sure that the ground is water-retentive. Do not overfeed with nitrogenous fertilizer. Prune to open up plants to air and sunlight.

POTASSIUM DEFICIENCY

Currant bushes growing on peaty or chalky soil may be stunted. The leaves may be small and turn blue-green before going brown at the margins, which curl. Fruit, although brightly coloured, is small and sparse. Apply sulphate of potash in spring at the rate of 100–150g/4–5oz per square metre/yard.

RASPBERRY VIRUS

All cane fruit is susceptible. The leaves of infected plants are yellow and distorted. The canes become stunted, and few fruits are produced. Dig up and burn the plants and plant new, certified virus-free canes in a different part of the garden. Control aphids, which spread the virus.

REVERSION DISEASE

This viral disease is carried by the big bud mite and affects blackcurrants. The leaves of infected plants are narrower than usual and have fewer lobes. It is more often identified when flowerbuds turn bright magenta (instead of grey), and bushes lose vigour and crop poorly. Control the mites that spread the disease. Dig up and burn infected bushes and plant certified disease-free stock in another part of the garden.

SPUR BLIGHT

This affects blackberries, loganberries and raspberries. In early summer new canes have purple blotches, which turn silver-grey and are covered with black fungal spots. Buds die or there is dieback in spring. Cut out and burn diseased canes as soon as the problem is noticed. Spray with a copper-based fungicide when buds open.

Tools and equipment

If you look in the average garden centre you would imagine that you need a tremendous battery of tools and equipment before you could ever consider gardening, but in fact you can start (and continue) gardening with relatively few tools and no equipment at all.

BUYING TOOLS

It is not necessary to buy a vast armoury of tools when you first start gardening. Most of the jobs can be done with a basic kit. When you are buying tools, always choose the best you can afford. Many of the cheaper ones are made of pressed steel, which soon becomes blunt and will often bend. Stainless steel is undoubtedly the best, but it tends to be expensive. Ordinary steel implements can be almost as good, especially if you keep them clean. Avoid tools that are made of aluminium. Trowels and hand forks especially are often made of aluminium, but they wear down and blunt quickly and are not good value for money.

A good pair of secateurs (pruning shears) will be essential for cutting back fruit bushes and canes. The two most popular types are bypass and anvil secateurs. Bypass secateurs have a sharpened, convex blade, which cuts against a broad concave or straight blade. As long as you keep the blades sharp, this type of secateurs cuts cleanly and is useful for getting into small, awkward corners.

Anvil secateurs have a straight blade that cuts against a flat anvil, which may, in expensive models, have a groove cut in it to allow sap to run away. The anvil is made of softer metal than the cutting blade to reduce the blunting effect. If you do not keep the cutting blade sharp this type of secateurs tends to crush the stem, rather than cutting it cleanly, and this can lead to pests or diseases entering the plant's tissues.

Some secateurs have a ratchet device built in, which is useful if you find ordinary secateurs difficult to work with and grip. The ratchet makes it possible to cut through a stem in several small movements, which require less effort than a single cut.

SOIL TESTERS

A range of soil testers are available for testing different aspects of soil quality. The most commonly used checks the pH (acidity/alkalinity) of the soil. It is chemical based and involves mixing soil samples with water and checking the colour against a chart.

CARE AND MAINTENANCE

Look after your tools. If you do this they will not only always be in tip-top working condition but should last a lifetime. Scrape all the mud and vegetation off the tools as soon as you have used them. Once they are clean, run an oily rag lightly over the metal parts. The thin film of oil will stop the metal from corroding. This not only makes the tools last longer but also makes them easier to use because less effort is needed to use a clean spade than one that has a rough, rusty surface.

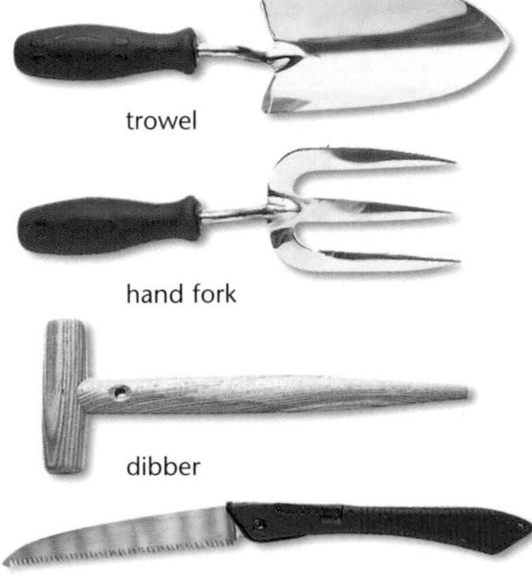

trowel

hand fork

dibber

pruning saw

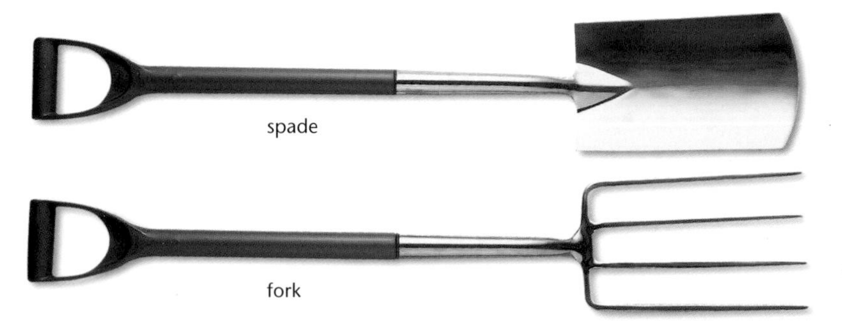

spade

fork

LABELLING AND TYING

When working in the garden, it is useful to have a tray of odds and ends, such as string, raffia, plant ties and labels. You never know when you might need them. For example, it is always difficult to remember what has been planted or sown where – it may be weeks before seed you have sown is visible above ground.

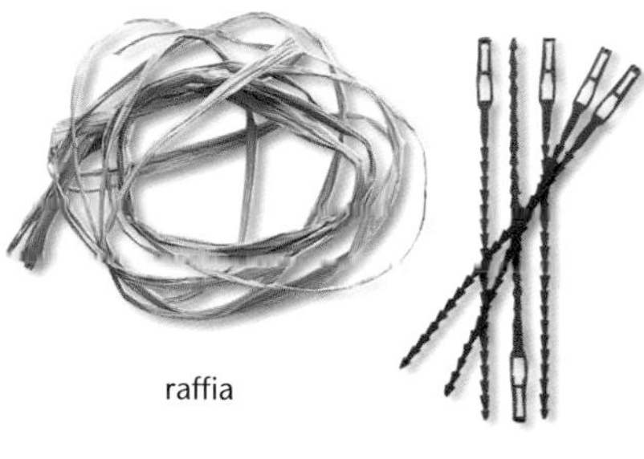

raffia

plant ties

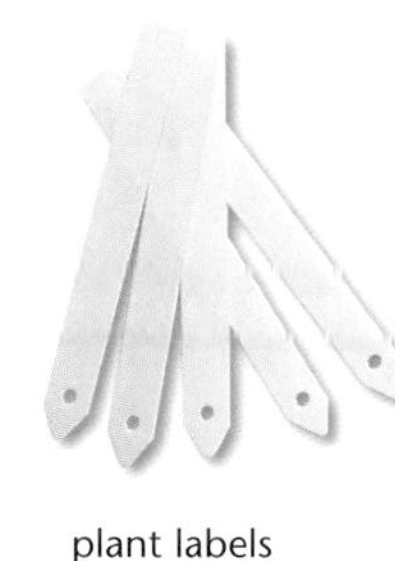

plant labels

twine

In addition, keep the wooden parts of tools clean, wiping them over with linseed oil if the wood becomes too dry. Keep all blades sharp and hang up tools in a dry place if possible to prevent corrosion. Standing spades and hoes on the ground, especially if it is concrete, will blunt them over time. Always keep all tools away from children.

EQUIPMENT

It is possible to maintain a fruit garden with no mechanical aids at all. Perhaps the only mechanical device that you may require is a rotavator (rototiller), which is used for digging and breaking up the soil, especially if you want to break down a heavy soil into a fine tilth. Keep all your equipment maintained in good working order. There is nothing worse than wanting a piece of machinery to use in a hurry only to find that it will not start.

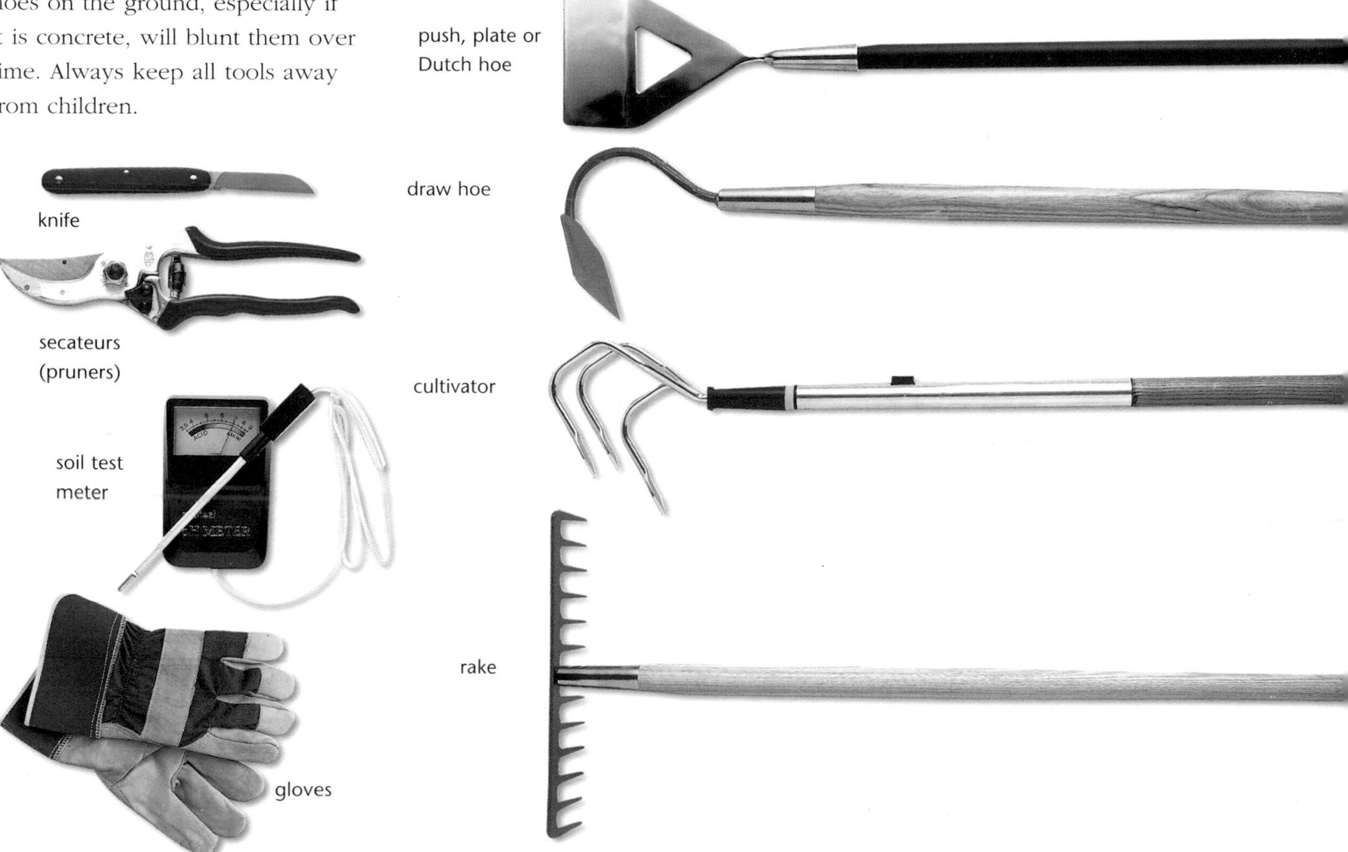

push, plate or Dutch hoe

draw hoe

cultivator

rake

knife

secateurs (pruners)

soil test meter

gloves

Growing strawberries

Strawberries are not very difficult to grow. If they are grown in beds they take up quite a bit of space, but they can also be grown in pots or in towers – a series of containers one on top of the other. They can be grown in a greenhouse, which produces earlier and later crops, but the flavour is not as good as that of crops grown outdoors.

The strawberry plants will remain productive for only about three years, and it is important to have a rolling programme to renew a third of the plants each year. Unfortunately, they really need to be planted in fresh ground, so it is not simply a question of taking out one row and replacing it with another; the new plants should ideally go elsewhere in the garden. Alternatively, you can create a completely new bed in the third year, and abandon the old one immediately after the strawberries have been harvested.

CULTIVATION

Strawberries need an open, sunny site. The soil should be fertile and well drained. The plants should be set out in late summer or early autumn, at intervals of 38cm/15in, with each row 75cm/30in apart. As the plants come into fruit the following year, place clean straw under the leaves and fruiting stems to keep the fruit off the ground. Plastic or felt mats will serve the same purpose. Water copiously during dry periods.

Strawberries can be planted through a sheet of black plastic, which acts as a mulch, keeping the soil beneath warm and moist. Dig over the area, incorporating well-rotted compost into the ground, and heap up the soil slightly in the centre of the area so that rainwater drains away from the plants.

ABOVE After fruiting, the strawberry plant sends out a series of runners that root along their length to produce new plants.

ABOVE After the strawberries have produced their fruit, cut off all the leaves and burn or destroy them, along with the straw mulch. This helps prevent the spread of diseases.

ABOVE The strawberry runners have produced a perfect new plant through layering. If you want to start a new bed, you can dig up the newly rooted plants and move them to a new site.

Water thoroughly, then place a piece of black plastic over the plot. Use soil or planks to hold down the edges of the sheet, make X-shaped cuts in the plastic and plant the strawberries through the holes.

PRUNING AND TRAINING

Strawberries are not pruned or trained as such, but after fruiting it is normal practice to cut off all the old leaves and burn or destroy these, together with the straw mulch, to remove any pests and diseases. Remove any runners as they are formed unless you want to keep a few new plants.

HARVESTING

Pick the fruit as it ripens. Pick with a short piece of stalk attached.

PESTS AND DISEASES

Birds and slugs are two of the worst problems. Birds can be kept at bay if the plants are netted while they are in fruit. Viruses and grey mould can also be problems. Burn any plant that becomes infected with a viral disease.

RIGHT Place a layer of straw under the leaves of the strawberry plants in order to prevent the developing fruit from getting muddy or covered with dirt.

ABOVE On this plant a succession of stages can be seen, from flowers to ripe fruit. The flavour of the fruit that is eaten as soon as it has been picked straight from the plant is unbeatable.

Growing raspberries

Raspberries are an appealing fruit, although they are often overshadowed by strawberries, which come into season at about the same time. They are excellent for eating straight from the plant or for freezing or making into jams and preserves. They can be used in a wide range of cakes and desserts as well as sauces for both sweet and savoury dishes.

It is possible to produce a good crop of raspberries by growing a group of just a few canes, but it is more usual to grow the canes in a row. This may take up quite a large amount of space, but it can be used as a hedge or screen, so fulfilling a double function. The canes are tied into wires that are supported on posts, which adds to the initial cost, but once the framework has been erected it will last for a long time, as will the raspberries themselves.

As with strawberries, new strains of raspberry have been developed so that it is possible to have a supply of fruit from early summer right through to the first frosts, which in a mild year can mean early winter. Rather than having three separate rows, which would take up a great deal of space, it is possible to divide a single row into three or even four separate sections for early, mid-season, late and autumn fruit.

CULTIVATION

Like most fruit, raspberries like an open situation with plenty of air circulating among them, but, unlike most other fruit, they will tolerate a little partial shade. The soil should be fertile and moisture-retentive, but it should not be waterlogged. Permanent supports in the form of posts and wires should be erected. The wires should be 75cm/30in, 1.1m/3ft 6in and 1.5m/5ft from the ground. Allow 1.5m/5ft between rows. Plant the canes at intervals of 38–45cm/15–18in, spreading out

BELOW This double row of raspberries is supported by wires that are secured on a well-constructed wooden framework.

RIGHT Ripening and immature fruit on a raspberry cane. Ripe raspberries can be obtained over a very long period if the varieties are chosen carefully.

their roots, during late autumn or early winter. Remove any suckers that appear out of the row, and use them as new stock if required.

PRUNING AND TRAINING

Each autumn remove all the old summer-fruiting canes by cutting them off at the base. Tie in the new canes to the wires. In late winter cut off the tip of each cane to a bud about 15cm/6in above the top wire. If you grow autumn-fruiting varieties, cut all canes to the ground in late winter.

HARVESTING

Pick as the fruit becomes ripe, squeezing gently with the fingers so that the fruit slides off its plug.

PESTS AND DISEASES

Birds are a nuisance unless the raspberry canes are netted or protected in a fruit cage. Raspberry beetle is often a nuisance. Spray with derris as soon as the first fruits begin to ripen, and then make a second application two weeks later. Botrytis or grey mould can cause the fruit to rot and there is also the possibility of some viral diseases. Infected canes should be removed and either burned or destroyed.

RIGHT Soft fruit, such as strawberries, raspberries and gooseberries should be picked between thumb and finger.

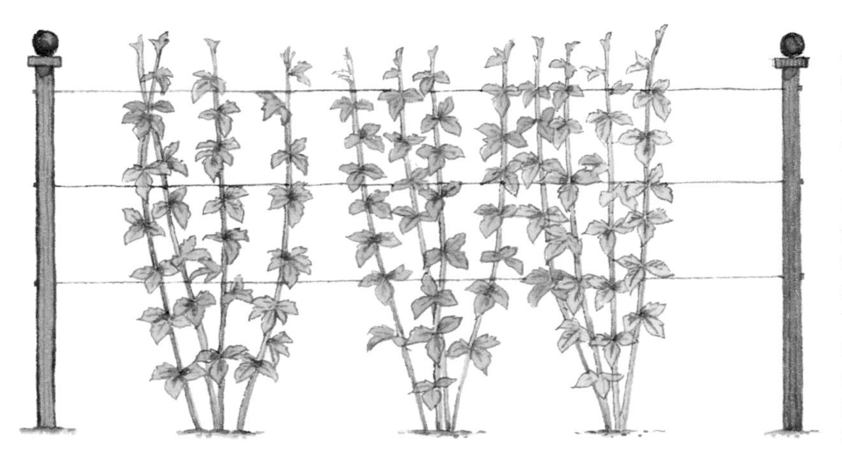

GROWING RASPBERRIES ON POSTS AND WIRES It is essential that raspberries have a strong supporting system of posts and wires. The plants are set at 38–45cm/15–18in intervals. Each year, new raspberry canes are thrown up. When fruiting has finished on the old canes, these are cut out and the new canes are tied to the wires in their place. This sequence is followed every year. Raspberry plants put out suckers, which can become established in the gangways between the rows. These should be dug up as soon as they appear.

Growing blackberries and hybrid berries

Although blackberries that are picked in the wild from brambles have a great deal to offer, there are advantages to be gained from growing cultivated forms. The first is that they are conveniently at hand. Second, the fruit is usually much larger and often sweeter. Then there is the fact that you can get thornless varieties, which makes picking much easier.

A disadvantage, however, is that they are vigorous plants and you do need quite a bit of space to grow them successfully, although they do not need to be a free-standing crop. They can, for example, be grown along a boundary fence, which may well be a convenient use of space as well as a good way of deterring intruders.

Cultivated blackberries are derived from their wild relatives; the hybrid berries are crosses between various *Rubus* species, often involving blackberries and raspberries in their parentage. Each of these berries, including loganberries, boysenberries and tayberries, has a distinctive flavour and is grown in the same manner as blackberries.

They come into fruit from late summer onwards and are available later in the year than most other soft fruit. Like most fruit, black-berries and hybrid berries are best eaten straight from the garden, but they can also be used in a wide range of dessert dishes and sauces.

Blackberries are usually grown on post and wire supports, the wires being placed at 38cm/15in intervals up to about 1.8m/6ft. The thornless varieties are not as vigorous and take up less space. In a really large garden, blackberries could be left to grow free, like their wild cousins, but this is not recommended because cultivated varieties are often much more vigorous than wild forms.

ABOVE Blackberries fruit over a long season, as is shown by this sprig of ripe and immature blackberries.

CULTIVATION

Blackberries prefer a sunny spot, but will grow in a modicum of partial shade. The soil should be well prepared, with plenty of added humus. Plant the canes in late winter or early spring, placing them 3.5–4.5m/12–15ft apart (thornless varieties can be closer together), and immediately shorten them to a bud about 23–30cm/9–12in above ground. Do not plant deeply; the soil should only just cover the roots, which should be spread out in the planting hole. Mulch with manure

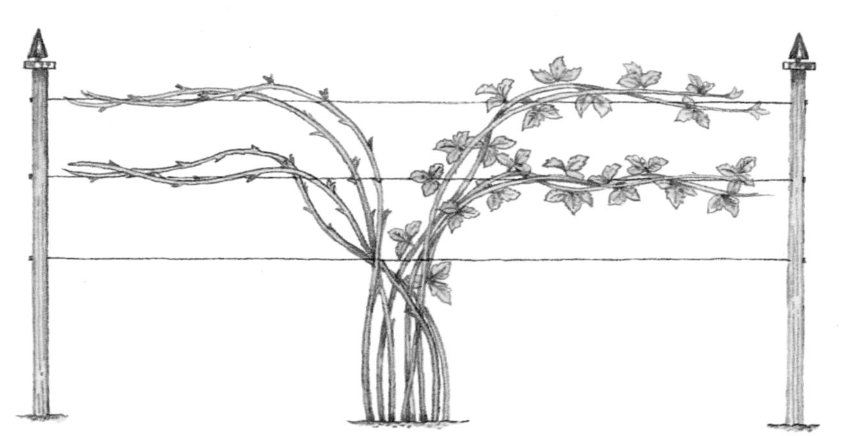

ALTERNATE BAY One way to train blackberries is to tie all the new growth to one side of the wirework. After fruiting, remove the previous year's growth from the other side and then use this for the next year's new growth. Repeat this each year.

ROPE TRAINING An alternative way to train blackberries is to temporarily tie in all new growth vertically to the wirework and along the top wire. The current fruiting canes are tied in groups horizontally. These are removed after fruiting and the new growth tied into their place.

in the spring and water in dry weather. They can be increased by bending down a vigorous shoot and planting its tip to form a layer. A new plant will quickly form and can be severed from the parent.

PRUNING AND TRAINING

In autumn cut out all the old fruiting stems and tie in the new growth. There are several methods of training blackberries and hybrid berries. One is to tie in all of one year's growth to one side, several canes to each wire, and the new growth to the other side. Another is to tie the fruiting growth along the wires, allowing new growth to grow up the centre. A formal and higher yielding method is to create a fan, with the shoots tied in a radiating pattern from the base, leaving the centre free for new growth.

The blackberry 'Himalayan Giant' does not produce new canes as freely as most other cultivars, and it crops well on canes that are two years old as well as on one-year-old canes. The best method of pruning this cultivar is to cut out those canes that have fruited twice.

HARVESTING

Pick the berries as soon as the fruit is ripe, without any stalks. Hold the berry between the first finger and thumb. The slightest of squeezes and slight pull and the fruit should fall into your upturned hand. It should come cleanly away from the stalk, which remains on the briar.

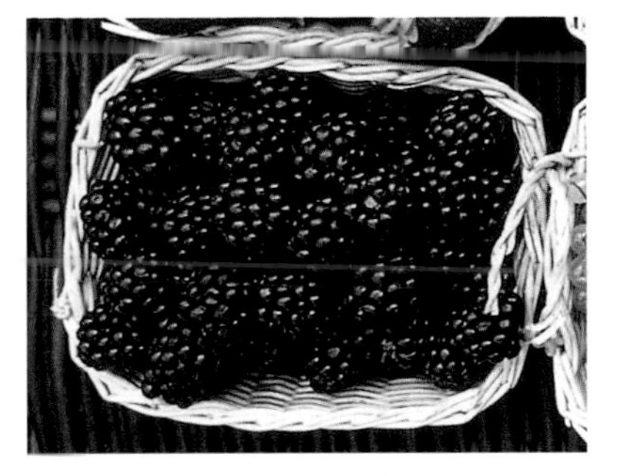

ABOVE Juicy, late summer fruiting blackberries are delicious fresh or cooked in preserves, puddings and cakes.

PESTS AND DISEASES

Blackberries are susceptible to the same problems as raspberries, including raspberry beetle maggots, which may be found in berries. They also sometimes suffer from botrytis (grey mould) and various viral diseases, although some disease-resistant strains are being developed. Netting may be needed to protect against birds.

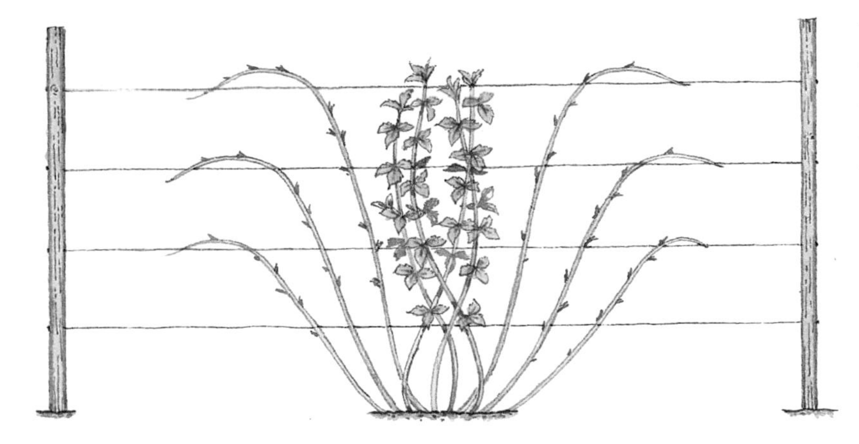

FAN TRAINING The new canes are temporarily tied vertically and along the top wire, while the fruiting canes are tied in singly along the wires. Any excess canes are removed. After fruiting, canes that have fruited are taken out and the new growth tied into their place.

Growing blueberries

The highbush blueberry is becoming more popular in the garden. The rich, fruity flavour that is a characteristic of the berries has made it popular as a fruit to be eaten straight from the bush and for inclusion in an ever-increasing number of desserts and other dishes. Its disadvantage as a garden fruit, at least for some people, is that it must have acid conditions, and for a good crop it needs a pH of between 4.0 and 5.5. In chalky or limestone (alkaline) regions bushes could be grown in large containers away from the normal garden soil, but this could become quite a chore, no matter how tasty the resulting berries.

The bushes and berries are decorative and are a useful addition in the potager or in an ornamental border or bed.

CULTIVATION

Choose a sunny site, although a little light, partial shade will be tolerated. The soil must be acidic with a soil pH of 4 and 5.5. Add ericaceous compost (soil mix) if your garden soil is just on the borderline or neutral. Set out the plants at any time the weather and soil conditions allow between autumn and early spring. Plant them as free-standing bushes, 1.5m/5ft apart. Mulch with manure, but only if it has not been sweetened with chalk or limestone. Do not allow the soil to become dry, watering regularly as necessary. Propagate from soft-wood cuttings taken in midsummer in cool climates or as hardwood cuttings in warmer climates.

PRUNING AND TRAINING

Blueberries are slow-growing bushes, and they require little pruning. Because they fruit best on branches that are two or three years old it is best not to prune them at all for the first three or four years. If you do, cut out any very weak growth or branches growing horizontally close to the soil.

In spring cut out weak or spindly growth. Initially this may be all that is required. On older plants, once a branch is becoming less productive, prune it out, preferably cutting it back to a point where there is a young replacement shoot. Otherwise, cut it back to its point of origin. At the same time prune out any badly placed shoots. Do not remove more than about a quarter of the branches at any one time.

HARVESTING

Pick as the fruit ripens and store, if necessary, by freezing or bottling.

PESTS AND DISEASES

The main problem with blueberries will be birds that will steal the fruit, but netting will solve this.

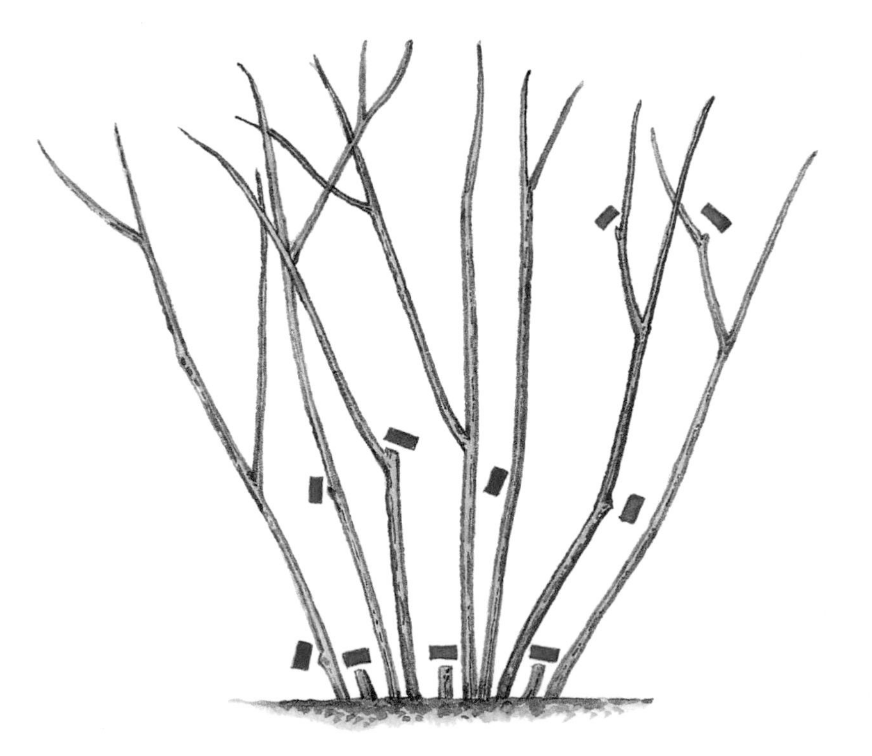

PRUNING AN ESTABLISHED BLUEBERRY BUSH Blueberries fruit on older wood, so no pruning is needed for several years. Thereafter, cut out any weak or misplaced shoots as well as the old wood that has ceased fruiting in order to stimulate new growth.

Growing cranberries

There are several related species of fruit that are known and grown as cranberries. They are all members of the genus *Vaccinium*. In America there is the large cranberry or American cranberry, *Vaccinium macrocarpon*, and it is these berries that are mainly seen in shops and in bought products such as cranberry sauce. They are also the most commonly available plants.

The small European cranberry, *V. oxycoccus*, is also widely grown. It produces smaller fruit with an acid, but pleasant, taste. A third form, also known as cranberry but more correctly called the cowberry, is *V. vitis-idaea*. This has small fruit that is acid to the taste and best used in cooking rather than eaten fresh. It can be cultivated, but generally the berries are harvested in the wild from the vast areas of moorlands and bogs that they grow on.

CULTIVATION

The type of soil in which cranberries are grown is important. It must be acid, with an ideal pH of 4.5, and it must be moist. Growing cranberries is a useful way of utilizing otherwise useless boggy ground or you can plant them in damp soil next to a pond. Cranberries grow in cool conditions and are extremely hardy, withstanding temperatures down to -45°C/-50°F, so they are best grown in northern temperate gardens. They can be grown in full sun or light shade. Plant at 60cm/2ft intervals, and they will spread to fill the gaps.

PRUNING AND TRAINING

No training is required and very little pruning. To keep the bushes compact they can be sheared over lightly once a year after fruiting, but generally they are best left to their own devices.

HARVESTING

Pick the berries as they ripen in the autumn and before the birds get them. They should all be harvested before the frosts as these will make them sour. The best method of storage is by freezing or by preserving, as in cranberry sauce. They can also be dried.

PESTS AND DISEASES

Generally cranberries are completely trouble-free. Birds taking the fruit is the biggest problem, but the low shrubs can be easily netted. If the plants fail to thrive it is most likely to be caused by lime in the soil or by too hot and dry conditions.

RIGHT A cranberry bush yields a whole basketful of fresh, ripe cranberries.

Growing gooseberries

Because most people think that gooseberries need cooking and so do not fit into the world of convenience foods, they are not, perhaps, as popular as they were in the past. This is a pity, partly because gooseberries have a very distinctive flavour, suitable for a range of dishes and sauces, but also because gooseberries can be eaten raw – there are some delicious dessert varieties. Unfortunately, these rarely find their way into shops, and so it is only gardeners who are likely to appreciate them – an excellent reason for growing your own.

Gooseberries are easy plants to grow, the only drawback being the thorns, which can be very sharp, but well-trained bushes and the use of cordons make it easier to get at the fruit without being torn to pieces. Typical gooseberries are green, but there are also red and yellow varieties.

CULTIVATION

Gooseberries require an open, sunny position, although they will take some light shade. The soil should contain lots of well-rotted organic material. Plant the bushes at any time between autumn and early spring when the weather and soil are favourable. They should be set 1.5m/5ft apart. Mulch in spring with a layer of manure. Avoid hoeing because the roots are only just below the surface and can be damaged. New plants can be propagated by hardwood cuttings taken in autumn.

ABOVE Gooseberries can be grown as single cordons. This is achieved by tying them in to canes which are supported by horizontal wires.

PRUNING AND TRAINING

Gooseberries can be grown as bushes, cordons or standards, but they are usually grown on a short leg (a length of clear stem). Alternatively, they can be grown as bushes that branch from the base. The main pruning is done in winter, but supplementary summer pruning is carried out to keep the bush open and well ventilated to reduce the risk of mildew and other diseases.

Gooseberry bushes are not difficult to prune, although the thorns can make the job unpleasant. In winter cut out any very low, badly placed or crossing branches. Aim to keep the centre of the bush as open as possible. Work over the bush to reduce the previous summer's growth at the end of each main shoot by between one-third and a half. Shorten sideshoots growing from the main stems, cutting them back to two buds from the old wood. After pruning the bush will retain its old shape and proportions, but the growth will be less cluttered and tangled.

Although summer pruning is not essential it helps to keep the bush open, increases air circulation and thereby reduces the risk of diseases, especially mildew. In midsummer cut any sideshoots back to five leaves from their base. Do not shorten the tips of the main shoots at this stage.

When they are grown as single, double or triple cordons the fruits are borne on spurs that grow directly from the main stem.

The size of dessert gooseberries can be increased by thinning in early summer. If alternate fruits are

ABOVE Cut out any low, badly placed or crossing branches. Work over the previous summer's growth at the end of each main shoot by between one-third and one-half.

ABOVE After pruning, the bush will retain its old shape and proportions, but the growth will be less cluttered and tangled. Wear gloves when pruning the bushes.

removed, the remaining berries will grow twice as large, and you can use the fruits you have removed in cooked dishes or for bottling.

HARVESTING

Start to harvest the berries just before they are quite ripe if you are going to cook or freeze them, but wait until they are wholly ripe if they are for eating raw. Continue picking as the fruit ripens, taking fruits with a stalk, but this has to be removed before they are stored. Gooseberries can be frozen, bottled or made into jams or other preserves.

PESTS AND DISEASES

On the whole, gooseberries are not prone to a great many pests and diseases. The main problems are American gooseberry mildew and gooseberry sawfly. One way to prevent mildew is to ensure that plenty of air can circulate around and through the bushes. There are mildew-resistant cultivars, such as 'Greenfinch'. Birds can also be a nuisance in spring when they strip off buds.

PRUNING A GOOSEBERRY The basic aim when pruning gooseberries is to create an open framework. Establish a framework, first of all, by removing the basal shoots and cutting back the main shoots by about half in their first and second years. After this, cut back the new growth on the leaders in winter by about half and reduce the sideshoots from these to two buds. Remove any damaged wood and any branches that cross or rub. Remove suckers and basal growth. In summer, prune the sideshoots back to five leaves, but leave the main stems uncut.

Growing blackcurrants

Blackcurrants have a unique flavour and are much valued for their high vitamin C content. They are used widely in desserts as well as jams and drinks. Like red- and whitecurrants, blackcurrants tend to have a relatively short season compared with other soft fruit, but although related to redcurrants they are pruned in a different way. Because the fruit is produced on the previous season's growth, it is important that this is not removed. Unlike redcurrants, blackcurrants can only be grown on bushes.

PRUNING A BLACKCURRANT BUSH After planting, cut the bushes back to a single bud above the ground. The following winter, remove any weak or misplaced growth. Subsequent pruning should take place after fruiting and consists of cutting out up to a third of two-year-old or older wood in order to stimulate new growth. Remove any weak or misplaced stems.

CULTIVATION

Blackcurrants prefer a sunny site, although they will tolerate a little light shade. The soil should be well prepared and have plenty of well-rotted humus added to it. Plant between autumn and early spring, setting the plants at intervals of 1.5m/5ft. Mulch in spring with a layer of well-rotted organic material. Water the bushes during dry spells but not when the fruit starts to ripen or it may split. Propagate from hardwood cuttings taken in autumn.

PRUNING AND TRAINING

After planting the bushes, reduce all the shoots to one bud above the ground. The following winter remove any weak wood. After that, continue each year to remove any weak wood and up to a third of the older wood, which should then stimulate the production of new growth. Never reduce the lengths of the shoots.

HARVESTING

The best and most nutritious fruit is always the crop you consume soon immediately after picking. Given kind weather and a certain amount of skill on the gardener's part, however, there should be sufficient fruit not only to supply the kitchen but also to store for later use and preserve.

LEFT Blackcurrants and redcurrants are usually picked in bunches, complete with their stalks.

Growing red- and whitecurrants

Red- and whitecurrants have a distinctive, tart flavour, but white-currants are slightly sweeter than the red. Redcurrants in particular are very attractive. They crop on short shoots that grow from a permanent frame of branches, and the bushes can be trained as standards, cordons or fans and used as a decorative feature. The fruiting season is comparatively short, around midsummer. As well as being used as fruit in their own right, both are frequently used as decoration on cakes and in a wide range of desserts and savoury dishes.

CULTIVATION

Both red- and whitecurrants prefer a sunny site and a rich, moisture-retentive soil. Plant between autumn and early spring at intervals of 1.2–1.5m/4–5ft. Cordons can be 30cm/12in apart, and fans can be 1.8m/6ft apart. Mulch in spring with well-rotted organic material. Propagate from hardwood cuttings taken in early autumn.

PRUNING AND TRAINING

Initially, prune back all main stems to four buds. After that, prune in spring and summer, reducing the growth on the new leader by about half and that on laterals to about 8cm/3in in spring and to four or five leaves in summer. Once the bushes are established, cut back all sideshoots to one bud and take the tip out of the main stems. Let new shoots from the base replace older wood. If you are growing them as cordons, in early spring remove a third of the new growth on the leader and cut back laterals to three buds. In summer cut back all laterals to five leaves.

ABOVE These cordons of red- and whitecurrants have been tied to vertical canes which are, in turn, tied to horizontal wires.

PESTS AND DISEASES

Birds attack both buds and fruit. Aphids, blackcurrant gall mites and grey mould may all cause problems, and coral spot can affect branches.

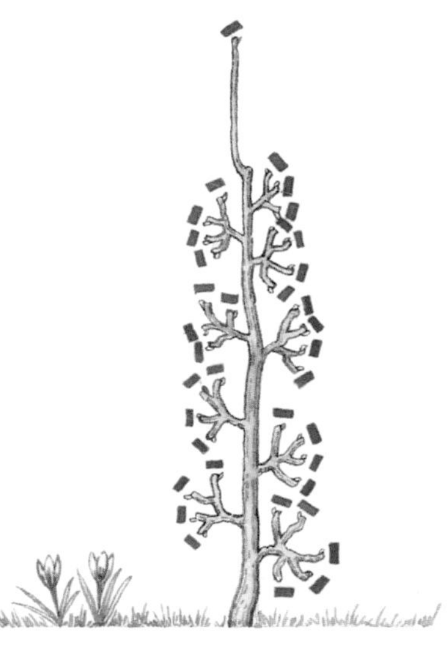

PRUNING A RED- OR WHITECURRANT CORDON On planting, cut back the leader by half of its new growth and cut back the sideshoots to one bud. Thereafter, cut back the sideshoots every summer to five leaves and, in winter, further reduce these to one bud.

PRUNING A RED- OR WHITECURRANT BUSH After planting, cut back each shoot by about half. Subsequent pruning involves ensuring that the plant becomes an open bush. Cut back all new growth on the main shoots and reduce the new growth on all sideshoots to one bud.

Growing elderberries

These deciduous shrubs and small trees are found in temperate and subtropical regions in hedgerows and woodlands and along roadsides in Europe, Africa, Australia and throughout North and South America. In Britain the common elder, *Sambucus nigra*, is often grown in the ornamental parts of the garden, but its attractive flowers and autumn berries have many practical uses. In the United States *S. canadensis*, the sweet elder, is usually grown.

Since the earliest times the elder has been associated with myth and magic and with witchcraft and spells, but its value in medicinal, household, culinary and cosmetic preparations has long been appreciated. Old herbals are filled with recipes for using the flowers, shoots, buds and berries, and distilled elderflower water was said to ensure a fair complexion.

It is a valuable plant for attracting wildlife to the garden. Robins, thrushes, blackbirds, dunnocks, wrens, tits, starlings and pigeons will appreciate the berries, while many pollinating insects are attracted to the summer flowers.

Left unpruned, elders make small trees, to 10m/33ft tall. They have dull green, pinnate leaves, divided into five elliptic leaflets. In early summer they bear flat umbels of creamy, musk-scented flowers. In early autumn these are followed by pendulous clusters of spherical black fruits on red stalks. There are several ornamental cultivars, which make attractive subjects for the garden but have no medicinal or culinary value. Only the black-berried elders are grown for fruit.

CAUTION
Elder leaves contain toxic cyanogenic glycosides and should not be eaten. The berries are harmful if eaten raw.

CULTIVATION

Elders grow in any well-drained soil, but they do best in humus-rich soil in sun or partial shade. The golden-leaved and variegated forms do best in full sun, but green-leaved elders are tolerant of sun or shade.

Plants can be propagated from hardwood cuttings, planted outdoors in winter, or from semi-ripe heel cuttings, which should be planted in summer in a greenhouse. Plants also produce suckers, which can be planted up. The species, but not cultivars, can be grown from seed sown in containers in autumn.

PRUNING AND TRAINING

If they are left unpruned elders eventually become untidy and unstable. It is possible to cut them hard back in winter, and they will reshoot, although flowers and fruits will be lost for a year.

Established elders will make more compact shrubs if you cut out about a third of the oldest stems in mid-spring. Prune immediately after flowering. However, do not prune for the first three years.

LEFT Elderberries have a distinctive flavour that attracts both humans and birds. The fruits are made into syrups for colds as they have anticatarrhal properties.

1 To keep the elder shrub compact, prune the thin branches that were produced in the previous year, cutting them back in mid-spring to the framework of old branches.

2 Cut the shoots that were produced in the previous summer to within about 5cm/2in of the old wood, taking it back to just above a pair of healthy buds.

3 After pruning the shrub will look rather mutilated, but it will soon recover as the new shoots grow quickly in warm spring weather. Pruning ensures the shrub remains a similar size.

HARVESTING

The berries ripen from mid- to late summer and should be picked late when they are dark and have a bloom on the skins. The elderflowers should be picked straight after opening, and can be used fresh or dried to make home-made beauty preparations.

ABOVE Elderflowers are not only attractive but can be used in food and drink recipes.

PESTS AND DISEASES

Elders are mainly trouble-free, although blackfly sometimes infest the young shoots and leaves; spray with dimethoate or heptenophos in spring. Mosaic virus may sometimes be a problem, and if so, the plants should be destroyed. Verticillium wilt, a fungal disease, sometimes affects plants, causing leaves to wilt on a few shoots. Branches eventually die back. Cut out infected shoots and branches and spray with carbendazim. Many different species of birds are attracted to elders.

The leaves of elder trees have insecticidal properties and are boiled in water to make sprays against aphids and other garden pests. Wear gloves when handling.

MULBERRY TREE

This weeping form *Morus alba* 'Pendula' is an ideal variety of mulberry to grow in a small space. The shiny, heart-shaped leaves turn yellow in autumn as the edible fruits ripen. Unfortunately, the fruits are not borne in abundance. Generally, the small tree or bush grows to about 4m/13ft, sometimes smaller.